GOLIATH NEVER WINS

BOOKS BY SAMUEL RODRIGUEZ

Goliath Never Wins
Persevere with Power
Power for Your Day Devotional
Your Mess, God's Miracle
Your Mess, God's Miracle Study Guide
Walk Out of Your Mess
Fresh Oil, Holy Fire, New Wine
Fresh Oil, Holy Fire, New Wine Study Guide
40 Days of Fresh Oil, Holy Fire, New Wine

GOLIATH NEVER WINS

5 ROCK-SOLID STRATEGIES FOR SLAYING YOUR GIANTS

SAMUEL RODRIGUEZ

Chosen
a division of Baker Publishing Group
Minneapolis, Minnesota

Published by Chosen Books
Minneapolis, Minnesota
ChosenBooks.com

Chosen Books is a division of
Baker Publishing Group, Grand Rapids, Michigan

Printed in the United States of America

Library of Congress Cataloging-in-Publication Data
Names: Rodriguez, Samuel, 1969– author
Title: Goliath never wins : 5 rock-solid strategies for slaying your giants / Samuel Rodriguez.
Description: Minneapolis, Minnesota : Chosen, a division of Baker Publishing Group, [2026]
Identifiers: LCCN 2025051486 | ISBN 9780800763022 cloth | ISBN 9781493440863 ebook
Subjects: LCSH: Success—Religious aspects—Christianity | Success—Biblical teaching | David, King of Israel
Classification: LCC BV4598.3 .R653 2026
LC record available at https://lccn.loc.gov/2025051486

Cover design by Dan Pitts

Baker Publishing Group publications use paper produced from sustainable forestry practices and postconsumer waste whenever possible.

26 27 28 29 30 31 32 7 6 5 4 3 2 1

To Pastor Reina and her remarkable team for pioneering the first ever National Hispanic Christian Mental Health Initiative. Thank you for proclaiming and living out the truth of 2 Timothy 1:7—empowering individuals, families, and communities to walk in faith, freedom, and wholeness. Your work elevates hope and healing across our nation and beyond.

CONTENTS

FOREWORD

Pastor Sam Rodriguez has inspired me with his overt spirituality, plentiful kindness, and wisdom. All are on florid display in his new book, *Goliath Never Wins*. His overriding lesson is contagious and one we need to learn every day of our lives if we are to retain our humility in the face of God's wisdom. It is that God decides, not us. That our superficial assessments of each other may not meet God's assessments, which of course determine the course of reality. As Pastor Rodriguez writes, "God quickly let Samuel know that His criteria didn't necessarily align with human assumptions and expectations."

Pastor Rodriguez lives in the real world. His confidence that we are given the tools we need to fight all our battles and win is not only true but also contagious. "No matter how large the giants you face, you can stand strong in the power of God's Spirit. You are already equipped with everything you need to overcome them!"

At the same time, Pastor Rodriguez cautions that the fight that must be won may not always be a slam dunk. "Staring down a bully is never easy," he writes. He points out that growing up as a Puerto Rican kid is part of what gives him the grit and determination to overcome. It is also what makes him so easy to like. He is a living incarnation of God's determination to put joy and courage in the world.

Rodriguez's understanding that we are all Davids in the face of the world's Goliaths is profound. Humility leads to holiness. Here is where we learn to rely on God to save us. "Once we acknowledge we haven't been able to slay this giant ourselves—and will also be unable to overcome such obstacles on our own moving forward—then we're ready to seek God's help."

Pastor Rodriguez is deeply impressed and motivated by David's successes in the face of all obstacles. Rodriguez draws from Scripture constantly in *Goliath Never Wins* in order to motivate others. As he writes, he is a uniter not a divider; he brings people together. And this book does the same. By the time you finish reading it, you are no longer the person you were when you started it.

Here again, one of the central lessons is also what can be used to correct division and set us on the road to true societal healing. As Rodriguez profoundly writes, "I fear that we spend more time attacking, insulting, and criticizing each other than we do focusing on the giants that stand threatening us. We go around pointing our fingers at the specks in other people's eyes rather than addressing the planks obstructing our own vision. We lose the big eternal picture and nitpick on irrelevant details and individual flaws."

This book is deeply inspiring and energizing—it expands our spiritual awareness, much as Pastor Rodriguez does through his sermons and his spreading the Word of God and love.

Marc Siegel, MD, clinical professor of medicine, NYU Langone Health;
medical director, *Doctor Radio*; senior medical analyst, Fox News;
author, *The Miracles Among Us: How God's Grace Plays a Role in Healing*

FIRST STONE

IDENTITY

Anointed to Slay Your Giants with Purpose

You did not choose me, but I chose you and appointed you so that you might go and bear fruit—fruit that will last—and so that whatever you ask in my name the Father will give you.

John 15:16

1

Anointed to Prove Hell Wrong

Living as God's Chosen

> God has chosen you and anointed you for His divine purposes. You are not defined by temporary drama—you are defined by your timeless destiny!

Proving who you really are is not always easy.

If you've ever moved to a new city or state, then you know establishing your new home requires verifying your identity. You might have to provide official identification in order to rent or purchase a home, start a new job, initiate utility services, or request mail delivery. Typically, you provide a birth certificate, driver's license, Social Security card, or passport as proof that you are who you say you are. With reliable evidence in hand, you demonstrate to the proper authorities the veracity of being the person identified by your legal name.

This process does not always run smoothly, of course. If your name happens to be one shared by numerous others, then verifying your distinct identity can be tricky. For example, a quick online search reveals that currently in the United State there are more than five thousand people named Samuel Rodriguez spread across nearly all fifty states. Based on my experiences with mistaken identity, I don't need internet access to know how problematic this moniker multiplicity can be. Over the years, others have confused me with an artist and illustrator who has the same name, as well as a restaurant owner, real estate agent, university professor, football player, and law enforcement officer—each named Sam Rodriguez.

You likely have your own experiences crossing paths with people who have the same or a very similar name as yours. Middle names and unique spellings can help distinguish you, but if you've ever changed your name, perhaps due to marriage or divorce or for professional reasons, then you know those previous versions of your name often follow you around and sometimes compound confusion about who you are.

Even when you're able to prove you are who you say you are, another problem often emerges—dealing with who *others* say you are. Often, this depends on the role you play in one another's lives and the context of your relationship. You might become known as someone's spouse, someone's parent, someone's *abuelo* or *abuela*, someone's coworker or colleague, or someone's boss or manager. Perhaps you become well known for the kind of work you do—an entrepreneur, stylist, influencer, retailer, sales rep, scientist, artist, or pastor.

Aspects of our identity often shift according to our seasons of life. I'll never forget the first time a waitress referred to me as "sir" and asked if I qualified for the over-fifty-five discount—and I wasn't even fifty yet! Becoming a new parent affects your identity and the way others see you differently than becoming a new grandparent. Moving into a larger home in a nicer neighborhood colors the way others see you just as becoming an empty nester and downsizing does.

Out of all the ways you can be identified, however, one way anchors all the others. *When you are chosen by God for His purposes, you are anointed with a new identity.* New to you, at least, because as God's anointed, you discover who you were made to be.

Masterpiece in the Making

When you consider who you are and how you identify yourself, it's natural to focus on externals. You may think of yourself as a man or woman at your current age, weight, and height with your particular color eyes and hair. You might identify with a certain ethnicity, race, and ancestral heritage. Based on how your family, peers, and friends have responded to you, as well as the assumptions and messages absorbed from your culture and media, you likely have aspects of your appearance you like as well as ones you wish you could change. You may believe your nose is too big, your jawline too soft, or your hips too wide. Even the most attractive and athletic people often seem to self-criticize some aspect of their appearance that others may not even notice.

While you're consistently conditioned to define yourself by your appearance, God focuses on more than just your body. He knew you before He formed you in your mother's womb and set you apart as His anointed before you were born (see Jeremiah 1:5). His eyes saw your unformed body, and He knew every detail about you, knitting you together to create someone fearfully and wonderfully made in His own divine image (see Psalm 139:13–16). Your Creator not only designed you for a unique purpose only you can fulfill but provides the means and the power for you to become that person! "For we are God's masterpiece. He has created us anew in Christ Jesus, so we can do the good things he planned for us long ago" (Ephesians 2:10 NLT).

No matter what challenges you may be facing in your life right now, you are God's masterpiece in the making. Even when you know these truths describe and define who you really are, you will still encounter challenges to living out your identity—and you're not alone. Just consider David, whose life not only demonstrates God's constant presence and anointing but also reveals the obstacles and struggles David experienced along the way. Considered in its entirety, the life of David provides a framework for how we discover who God made us to be and how we live out His anointed purpose for our lives.

Over the course of his life, David received three divine anointings, with each one marking a crucial stage in his personal development and journey of faith. David was first anointed by the prophet Samuel as God's chosen successor to the throne of Israel (see 1 Samuel 16:13). Years later, David was anointed as king of Judah (see 2 Samuel 2:4) before finally being anointed as king over all of Israel (see 2 Samuel 5:3). I'm convinced these milestones are not merely historical events but are symbolic of the spiritual empowerment that every believer, through Christ's finished work, can experience in his or her calling.

Exploring the intricate moments of David's life, we see how his legacy is defined by three monumental accomplishments, each a testament to his respective anointings: defeating the giants of his generation, conquering and restoring Jerusalem, and bringing the Ark of the Covenant—the glory of God—into the heart of the city. Through David's victories, we can draw parallels to our lives today, affirming that we, too, are anointed through Christ to defeat the giants of our generation, to occupy the promises of God, and to bring His glory into the world.

Throughout these pages, we will delve deeply into the life of David and explore five key themes—identity, intimacy, integrity, influence, and innovation—as the foundation for how we can know, grow, and fulfill our divine destiny as God's chosen. Like the five stones that David selected in order to defeat Goliath, these five themes reveal how we can embody similar principles through the power of the Holy Spirit. Collectively, these five stones form a firm foundation for living out the divine destiny of our anointing.

These five stones also serve as a testament of God's power at work in our lives. Just as David faced doubters, detractors, and destructors who did their best to discourage him from living out his anointing, we often face obstacles, enemies, and critics in our way. When we have the resurrection power of God's Spirit in us, however, our response to all naysayers must also echo David's: "Watch me! You say I'm too young, too inexperienced, too naive to slay a giant? Just watch me! You say that I'm not good enough, smart enough, talented enough, or spiritual enough to overcome that barrier? Watch me!"

As we unfold David's story together, we will consider each element of his life within the context of Christ's finished work, revealing the timeless truths of God's anointing, His power to transform, and His purpose for each of us as individuals and as a body of believers. Others may not believe we have what it takes, but we know God has more than what it takes—and He has chosen us. Goliath never wins because you are anointed and equipped to slay your giants.

Just as God did with David, He has chosen you and anointed you to prove hell wrong!

Anointed as God's Chosen

Just as David observed in the psalms he wrote, your relationship with God began long before you were born. God knew you intimately prior to when you accepted His free gift of salvation through the death and resurrection of His Son, Jesus. Your Creator made you in His image to fulfill a mission on earth that only you can accomplish. He chose you before you chose Him! "We love because he first loved us" (1 John 4:19). Once you respond to His love and welcome the gift of the Holy Spirit into your life, you activate the divine calling God has placed on you. Embracing your identity as God's chosen results in His anointing through the power of His Spirit.

This process of discovering your identity and God's divine direction for your life rarely conforms to our human expectations—both those of the people around us as well as our own. We see this in David's life when he was first anointed by Samuel, marking David as God's chosen king, while he was still a young shepherd in his father's house. It's important to understand, however, that David was not the obvious candidate at the time for such a significant leadership role. Looking at what led up to David's selection, we notice that others—including his own family—overlooked him.

> The Lord said to Samuel, "How long will you mourn for Saul, since I have rejected him as king over Israel? Fill your horn with oil and be on your way; I am sending you to Jesse of Bethlehem. I have chosen one of his sons to be king."
>
> But Samuel said, "How can I go? If Saul hears about it, he will kill me."
>
> The Lord said, "Take a heifer with you and say, 'I have come to sacrifice to the Lord.' Invite Jesse to the sacrifice, and I will show you what to do. You are to anoint for me the one I indicate."

Samuel did what the LORD said. When he arrived at Bethlehem, the elders of the town trembled when they met him. They asked, "Do you come in peace?"

Samuel replied, "Yes, in peace; I have come to sacrifice to the LORD. Consecrate yourselves and come to the sacrifice with me." Then he consecrated Jesse and his sons and invited them to the sacrifice.

When they arrived, Samuel saw Eliab and thought, "Surely the LORD'S anointed stands here before the LORD."

But the LORD said to Samuel, "Do not consider his appearance or his height, for I have rejected him. The LORD does not look at the things people look at. People look at the outward appearance, but the LORD looks at the heart."

Then Jesse called Abinadab and had him pass in front of Samuel. But Samuel said, "The LORD has not chosen this one either." Jesse then had Shammah pass by, but Samuel said, "Nor has the LORD chosen this one." Jesse had seven of his sons pass before Samuel, but Samuel said to him, "The LORD has not chosen these." So he asked Jesse, "Are these all the sons you have?"

"There is still the youngest," Jesse answered. "He is tending the sheep."

Samuel said, "Send for him; we will not sit down until he arrives."

So he sent for him and had him brought in. He was glowing with health and had a fine appearance and handsome features.

Then the LORD said, "Rise and anoint him; this is the one."

So Samuel took the horn of oil and anointed him in the presence of his brothers, and from that day on the Spirit of the LORD came powerfully upon David. Samuel then went to Ramah.

1 Samuel 16:1–13

Notice that even Samuel, God's messenger and spokesman in this selection process, had his own expectations about the person the Lord had chosen. "Surely the LORD's anointed stands here before the LORD," Samuel thought when he saw Jesse's oldest son, Eliab. We aren't told what Eliab looked like or why Samuel assumed that he was the one. Eliab may have been tall and handsome with a certain regal bearing and kingly self-confidence about him. Samuel might have assumed the Lord had chosen Eliab because he was the eldest son, the primary heir of his father's household.

Whatever the reason, God quickly let Samuel know that His criteria didn't necessarily align with human assumptions and expectation. "Do not consider his appearance or his height, for I have rejected him. The Lord does not look at the things people look at. People look at the outward appearance, but the Lord looks at the heart" (1 Samuel 16:7). Read that verse once more slowly. It's not how you look. It's not your size. *It's your heart!*

God's response here sums up His divine hiring policy seen throughout the pages of Scripture. God selects His chosen sons and daughters and anoints them for their divine mission based on what remains *invisible to human eyes*. The Lord looks at our hearts and our willingness to love and serve Him, to trust Him daily for the rest of our lives, to rely on Him as the source of our power for doing what we could never accomplish in our own abilities. He knows us and what He has designed us to do, even if we don't seem particularly qualified or equipped based on the logical, rational criteria of human beings.

Others cannot see all that God sees in you!

Posture of Your Heart

People like to choose and elevate others—from pastors to presidents, social media stars to CEOs—based on their looks, their image, their brand, their vibe. People want to have confidence that those men and women chosen for positions of leadership and authority have the experience, the gravitas, and the fortitude to endure the rigors and challenges they will inevitably face. While we may be tempted to view this tendency as shallow, let's remember that our brains are wired to make quick assessments in order to help us survive, to know whom to trust and whom to fear. It's natural to want leaders who display charisma, embody strength, and exude power.

So we make assessments based on appearances, impressions, and our subjective perceptions. We often choose others—friends, employees, neighbors, teachers, colleagues, pastors, associates, mentors, spouses—based on who's the strongest, the smartest, the richest, the prettiest, the funniest, the most talented, the most eloquent, the most educated, or the most spiritual. Based on David's selection process, however, we see that God often rejects these same candidates no matter how poised, perfect, and powerful they may appear to be. Instead, the Lord looks at what's inside us, in our heart, our character, our feelings, our instincts, our attitudes, and our willingness to trust Him and trust in Him.

God has always chosen people based on what He sees in their hearts. The posture of your heart determines whether you're ready to assume His divine anointing. Throughout the Bible, again and again, we see that God selects people for His purposes based on criteria that people cannot see. His chosen leaders, movers, and shakers are the men and women willing to depend on Him in order to serve, stand firm, and overcome adversity. From Genesis to Revelation, the focus is never on perfect people but on unlikely underdogs who are chosen, anointed, and empowered by God.

God chose Noah to build an ark, load up the animals, and continue the human race.

God chose Abraham to be the forefather of His chosen nation.

God chose Joseph and used his betrayal by his brothers to save countless lives.

God chose Moses to confront Pharaoh and lead the Israelites out of Egypt.

God chose Joshua to conquer his own fears before conquering the city of Jericho.

God chose Rahab to help Joshua and the Israelites infiltrate Jericho.

God chose Gideon to defeat the Midianites.

God chose Samson to bring the temple down on the Philistines.

God chose David to slay Goliath, succeed Saul, and rule Israel.

God chose Esther to save the Jewish people.

God chose Daniel to tame the lions—and the Babylonians.

God chose the Hebrew boys to keep their cool in the fiery furnace.

God chose Peter to be the rock upon which He built His Church.

God chose Paul to preach the Gospel to the world.

And God chose to send His only and beloved Son, Jesus Christ, to live on earth and die on the cross to pay for all our sins once and for all, to rise from the grave and defeat death through the power of the Holy Spirit—the same Spirit that dwells in you!

What has God chosen you to do?

You may know exactly what He has created and called you to do, or you may be at the beginning of your divine discovery. Regardless of where you may be in your spiritual journey, regardless of circumstances and how things appear, regardless of the distance between where you are and where you are called to go, here's what I know is true: *God has created you as His beloved son or daughter for an earthly mission with eternal impact*. No matter how many giants you're facing, how many barriers stand in your way, how many others say you're not qualified or good enough, how many wounds linger from the past—you are the one God has chosen to do what no one else can do! You are the one He has anointed through the power of the Holy Spirit to do what only He can do through you.

After the Lord revealed His choice to Samuel, He instructed the prophet to anoint the young shepherd as a sign and seal of God's selection and His presence in David's life. Similarly, we see Jesus' first anointing at His baptism by John the Baptist where the Holy Spirit descended on Him like a dove, publicly affirming His identity as the Son of God.

> As soon as Jesus was baptized, he went up out of the water. At that moment heaven was opened, and he saw the Spirit of God descending like a dove and alighting on him. And a voice from heaven said, "This is my Son, whom I love; with him I am well pleased."
>
> Matthew 3:16–17

As the Son of God, Jesus did not need this anointing in order to fulfill the mission His Father sent Him to earth to accomplish. But God wanted those watching Jesus to know His Son's true identity. God wanted to reinforce the process displayed when David was chosen, which He continues to fulfill in the lives of His chosen sons and daughters. Both David and Jesus were chosen by God, and their anointings were a public declaration of God's special purpose for them. Just as David and Jesus were chosen, we, too, are chosen by God to fulfill His purposes in our lives.

God's Super over Your Natural

What is your true identity? What defines you more than how you look or what you've experienced? What determines and empowers you to live out of your God-given purpose? God's anointing anchors your identity. When the image of God encounters the Spirit of God, the purpose of God will come to pass!

You are not defined by your failures; you are defined by His forgiveness.

You are not defined by your trauma; you are defined by His testimony.

You are not defined by your drama; you are defined by His destiny.

You are not defined by the hell you're going through; you are defined by the heaven you are going to.

You are not defined by what you do for God; you are defined by what God already did for you.

Just like David, but upgraded exponentially through the finished work of Jesus Christ on the cross, you and I are anointed not to take selfies, not to occupy space, not just to survive, not to accommodate the false notions of silent Christianity, comfortable Christianity, or private Christianity. We proclaim with the psalmist, "I have been anointed with fresh oil" (Psalm 92:10 NKJV). And why are we anointed? *We are anointed with fresh oil to prove hell wrong!*

Your anointing is heaven's authority upon your divine assignment.

Your anointing is God's power to fulfill His purpose.

Your anointing is God's presence that enables you to occupy His promises.

Your anointing is God's super over your natural, enabling you to experience the supernatural.

Your anointing is when the grace, gift, and glory of God inside of you come together, empowering you to change the world in front of you.

God's Word records how His anointing has always allowed us to be conduits of His power and agents of change here on earth. "And they cast out many demons, and anointed with oil many who were sick, and healed them" (Mark 6:13 NKJV). We're reminded "how God anointed Jesus of Nazareth with the Holy Spirit and power, and how he went about doing good and healing all who were under the power of the devil, because God was with him" (Acts 10:38). From the first page to the last page in Scripture, throughout human history and still today at this very moment, we see that God uses His anointed to spread the Good News of the Gospel and to advance His Kingdom. Under the anointing . . .

We shout down walls.
We bring down giants.
We pray down fire.
We cast out devils and demons.
We lay hands on the sick and they recover.
We speak truth with love.
We pursue righteousness.
We show our children how to pray.
We advance the Lamb's agenda.
We promote justice, love mercy, and walk humbly before God.

Under the anointing, we embrace the One who is *invincible* as we believe for the *impossible* and accomplish the *incredible*!

My friend, you have been chosen and anointed for great things. You have been chosen and anointed to prove hell wrong by promoting heaven on earth.

You are saved.
You are delivered.
You are healed.
You are chosen.
You are anointed!

Selecting Your Stone

At the end of each chapter, you will find a few questions to help you reflect on the main points covered and how they apply to your life. These questions aren't here to burden you with homework but to enhance how you engage with and apply the main points of each chapter to your life. While you don't have to write down your responses, you might be surprised to discover how helpful it can be to keep a record of your relationship with God and how the Holy Spirit speaks to you as you read each chapter.

After you've spent a few moments reflecting on these questions, I encourage you to pray and share with God whatever has been stirred in your heart. To help ignite your conversation with the Lord, I have written a short prayer that you'll find after the questions. Regardless of whatever you may be facing in your life, trust that God is with you in the midst of it. He has created you for a divine purpose and anointed you with His Spirit to empower your journey, just as He did with David. You are God's beloved whom He has chosen and anointed for great things!

1. How would you describe your identity to someone who doesn't know you? What causes you to struggle with seeing yourself the way God sees you?

2. What do you already know about the life of David in the Old Testament? What thoughts and feelings stir within you when you consider that you have been chosen and anointed for God's purposes just as David was?

3. What barriers have been getting in the way of growing closer to God? How does knowing you are chosen and anointed by His Spirit empower you to overcome the obstacles in your life?

Dear God, You know me better than I know myself, and You created me for a divine mission that I continue to discover and live out. Thank You for choosing me and anointing me to be all that You created me to be so that I can have a positive impact on the lives of those around me. Allow me to prove hell wrong and to overcome the enemy's snares that prevent me from knowing and living fully in my true identity. Give me eyes to see and ears to hear as I explore the life of David and apply the truths of his experience to my own life. Empower me through Your Spirit with confidence and security in being all You want me to be. In Jesus' name, Amen.

2

Facing Goliath

Standing Firm in the Face of Opposition

No matter how large the giants you face, you can stand strong in the power of God's Spirit. You are already equipped with everything you need to overcome them!

Staring down a bully is never easy.

Growing up as a Puerto Rican kid in a working-class neighborhood in Pennsylvania, I quickly learned to keep my head down. I realized at an early age that I looked different, sounded different, and navigated the world differently than most of my peers. Some of them had no trouble accepting me while others seemed suspicious and antagonistic toward anything and anyone distinct from themselves. A few times I definitely encountered bullying, mostly with derogatory verbal epithets and juvenile threats.

This kind of bullying seemed to go with the territory and could largely be ignored. While their words definitely stung, I knew from observing the way my parents handled others' prejudiced attitudes that I should develop a thick skin. On a handful of occasions, I endured physical altercations, mostly shoving and pushing, that required me to stand up for myself. Despite being smaller and shorter than my would-be assailants, I realized that my defiance garnered their respect, which in turn alleviated the confrontation.

Not all bullying resulted from my classmates, however. Unfortunately, some adults I encountered used their positions of authority to "keep me in my place." I recall one high school guidance counselor who responded to my college applications and career goals with condescension and skepticism. Rather than helping me fulfill my academic and intellectual potential, this counselor advised me to focus on manual labor, such as landscaping or construction, the stereotypical roles for most Hispanic young men at the time.

Fortunately, I could ignore this adult's bullying with the same resolve I had employed to ignore the hurtful words on childhood playgrounds. But I also realized in this experience the one thing bullies all seem to have in common—the desire to exert power over others who threaten or intimidate them in some way. This demonstration of power allows bullies to hide their own insecurities at the expense of exposing someone else's. As long as they can maintain control—either physically or emotionally or both—over someone they perceive as different, then their fears of being less-than will remain buried.

I also realized one other important truth about bullies: They collapse when confronted by someone outraged by injustice.

Mind Games

Now I'm not saying that bullies always lose or that their weaknesses always get exposed. Sadly enough, bullies often appear to win temporarily, which only reinforces the use of these same tactics moving forward. Once they've intimidated, humiliated, or annihilated their target, they tend to repeatedly use their size, strength, authority, wealth, power, or title to cover up their weaknesses and elevate their egos.

Eventually, however, they encounter someone who refuses to back down. Someone who sees through their bravado and arrogance and stands up to them. Someone unafraid of confrontation. Someone unwilling to allow the bully to continue taunting, terrorizing, and torturing others.

Someone like David.

Of all the many feats of faith for which David is known, slaying the giant Philistine named Goliath is perhaps his best known. And since we know the ending—spoiler alert—of this ultimate underdog story, we might be tempted to assume their confrontation was fairly simple and straightforward. This assumption is valid if we only focus on that moment when a courageous shepherd boy slings a smooth stone with all his might into the forehead of an overconfident opponent and sends him crashing to the ground.

There's so much leading up to that moment, however, that must not be overlooked—not if we want to experience the same supernatural power required to confront the similar kinds of obstacles we face. Because even when we know we're called to take a stand, even when we plant ourselves firmly on the foundation of our steadfast faith in the living and almighty God, even when we know that everything in our lives has prepared us for this showdown, we will still encounter resistance.

Not just internally, not just from the giant taunting us, but externally from those who doubt us, resent us, and underestimate us. Self-doubt, fear, and anxiety might be natural responses when faced with a seemingly impassable barrier, so when you muster the courage and feel compelled to take a stand, you appreciate supportive reinforcement from others. Unfortunately, though, when an obstacle blocks their path as well, they may resent you for even trying. They play into the bully's mind games of manipulation and reinforce the impossibility of overcoming him or her. Such is the case with the formidable foe faced by the army of Israel.

> Now the Philistines gathered their forces for war and assembled at Sokoh in Judah. They pitched camp at Ephes Dammim, between Sokoh and Azekah. Saul and the Israelites assembled and camped in the Valley of Elah and drew up their battle line to meet the Philistines. The Philistines occupied one hill and the Israelites another, with the valley between them.
>
> A champion named Goliath, who was from Gath, came out of the Philistine camp. His height was six cubits and a span. He had a bronze helmet on his head and wore a coat of scale armor of bronze weighing five thousand shekels; on his legs he wore bronze greaves, and a bronze

> javelin was slung on his back. His spear shaft was like a weaver's rod, and its iron point weighed six hundred shekels. His shield bearer went ahead of him.
>
> Goliath stood and shouted to the ranks of Israel, "Why do you come out and line up for battle? Am I not a Philistine, and are you not the servants of Saul? Choose a man and have him come down to me. If he is able to fight and kill me, we will become your subjects; but if I overcome him and kill him, you will become our subjects and serve us." Then the Philistine said, "This day I defy the armies of Israel! Give me a man and let us fight each other." On hearing the Philistine's words, Saul and all the Israelites were dismayed and terrified.
>
> 1 Samuel 17:1–11

Notice the details provided in this description. First, we're given a tactical perspective, one that identifies not only the two warring armies but also their geographic location. Based on this big-picture, almost aerial viewpoint, they've apparently reached a standoff with each army occupying a hill framing the Valley of Elah between them.

From this overview, the focus then shifts to the real reason these two encampments are at a stalemate—because of the Philistine champion named Goliath. While it would have been simple to describe him as a giant or towering, this description lingers on details of dimension to make sure we understand the full power and might of this warrior. We're told he was over nine feet tall and wore a bronze helmet along with bronze armor weighing about 125 pounds. His legs were also protected by bronze armor, and he was armed with both a javelin and a spear, with the spearhead weighing roughly 15 pounds. This giant warrior also had a shield, which was carried by a servant ahead of him.

While the name Goliath has come to be synonymous with any enormous obstacle or giant opponent, its Hebrew origin reveals the root words *galah*, meaning "to expose" or "to reveal," and *galut*, which means "exile" or "captive." Both of these derivations emphasize that Goliath from Gath was a revelation that could not be ignored, an exile who literally stood above his tribe and any group of people he encountered.

Goliath clearly enjoyed using his stature as status. He couldn't resist shouting at the Israelites, questioning their apparent tactical paralysis, and reducing this military conflict to a one-on-one winner-take-all title bout in which he would fight any contender willing to step up. Leaving no room for doubting his boastful challenge, this giant Philistine declared, "I *defy* the armies of Israel!" (1 Samuel 17:10, emphasis added).

The combination of his size and arrogance had the impact Goliath desired, because we're told, "Saul and all the Israelites were dismayed and terrified" (1 Samuel 17:11). Consider this for a moment. The king and leader of the entire army of Israel—along with every soldier in his camp—felt overwhelmed with their impending defeat. They were not just afraid—they were *terrified*. They were not just intimidated—they were *dismayed*. As he was so accustomed to doing, Goliath had seemingly won the fight before it began.

Until a young, inexperienced, naive shepherd stepped forward—David.

Larger Than Their Actual Size

We all have giants like Goliath in our lives, enormous challenges that seem to loom over us no matter where we turn. Debt, cancer, divorce, addiction, past abuse and trauma—whatever has tried to defeat you through sheer size and undeniable power. It might be an ongoing battle with alcohol, substances, or prescription meds. You might have been in recovery several times and experienced seasons of freedom that proved only to be temporary before your next fall. You might be facing a mountain of debt—school loans, medical bills, credit cards—that seems impenetrable and unconquerable. No matter how much you try to stay on budget, to save, to focus on paying down the debt, something always seems to come up, some essential expense or costly need that cannot be ignored or denied—car repairs, unexpected surgery, the needs of your children.

These giants become animated by the enemy of your soul in an attempt to take you out of the fight. The devil wants you to feel defeated and afraid so that you won't keep trying, keep getting up again, keep asking for help, or keep trusting God. The enemy loves to make our giants appear larger than they really are. Jesus contrasted the purpose of the enemy with His own reason. "The thief comes only to steal and kill and destroy; I have come that they may have life, and have it to the full" (John 10:10). God's Word also warns us, "Your enemy the devil prowls around like a roaring lion looking for someone to devour" (1 Peter 5:8).

The giants in your life aren't simply barriers keeping you immobilized by fears and intimidation. They're being used by the enemy as spiritual blockades to hinder your growth and undermine your relationship with God. Not only are you fighting a battle against addiction or cancer or debt—you're fighting a spiritual battle as well. Paul explains, "For our struggle is not against flesh and blood, but against the rulers, against the authorities, against the powers of this dark world and against the spiritual forces of evil in the heavenly realms" (Ephesians 6:12).

Who and what are the Goliaths in your life?

What seemingly unconquerable addiction or persistent habit continues to tempt you?

How does the enemy of your soul prey on your weaknesses and use these giants to try to defeat you?

To terrify and discourage you?

To taunt and intimidate you?

To get in your head so that you feel defeated before you even attempt to fight?

To tilt you toward despair and hopelessness?

What obstacle have you allowed to bully you and rob you of joy, peace, and purpose?

It's important to identify these giants in your life and examine how and why they intimidate and frighten you. And it's essential that you recognize the spiritual battle that's taking place as well. But it's even more important to recognize the power you have to defeat these giants—resurrection power from the Spirit of God, the same Spirit who raised Jesus from the dead!

Humility Leads to Holiness

David's willingness to confront an enemy despite the incredible size differential reminds us that the first step is taking a stand. It's important to realize, however, that taking a stand against the Goliath in your life requires more than what you can muster on your own. There's a reason these giants continue to loom and taunt you—often because we keep fighting by ourselves until we're so exhausted we give up and give in. The devil knows that if he can convince us to try harder, work longer, push through by white-knuckling it on our own, then sooner rather than later we will fall.

Taking a stand against Goliath requires a supernatural power source.

If you've participated in a 12-step program or helped support someone in recovery, then you may know the first step. "We admitted we were powerless over [alcohol, narcotics, whatever addictive substance or behavior is causing the struggle] and that our lives had become unmanageable." Without acknowledging our weakness, it's difficult to access God's power in us. Defeating the giants in our lives begins with humility.

Humility leads to holiness. Once we acknowledge we haven't been able to slay this giant ourselves—and will also be unable to overcome such obstacles on our own moving forward—then we're ready to seek God's help. It's no coincidence then that the second step builds on our humility as we seek God's power to overcome what we cannot overcome on our own. "We came to believe that a Power greater than ourselves could restore us to sanity." If we want restoration, we need resurrection power that only God provides through His Spirit in us. No matter what giant we're facing, we must step out in faith despite our fears, insecurities, anxiety, and past mistakes.

You don't need to be in recovery or working a 12-step program to learn from this two-part method of taking a stand against your Goliath. People battling addictions know they cannot win this battle on their own. Followers of Jesus Christ should be even more aware of their need for relying on God and His Spirit within them to triumph over the giants in their path. We can resign ourselves to defeat, we can keep trying to slay our giants in our own power, or we can rely on God and take a stand.

Willing to Step Up

This is the example we see when David arrived on the scene and realized what was at stake. While David's three oldest brothers had enlisted and remained encamped at the battlefront, David, being the youngest, stayed home to tend their father's sheep and run errands back and forth (see 1 Samuel 17:15). So after Goliath had immobilized the Israelites with his taunts for forty days (see 1 Samuel 17:16), David's father, Jesse, told him to take some bread and cheese to his brothers and the commanders of their unit and see how the battle was progressing.

Only, there was no battle. There was just a standoff between Goliath and the fear of the Israelite army, which apparently continued to attempt taking battle positions and shouting their war cry (see 1 Samuel 17:20) before seeing Goliath and running away in great fear (see 1 Samuel 17:24). It's significant that the Israelite army tried to go through the motions of their military training, taking positions and shouting the war cry, but their fear of death and defeat at the hands of this giant kept them out of the battle. In other words, they were relying on their own power rather than the power of God.

David couldn't help but notice the way Goliath seemed to control the situation. The Philistine warrior had immobilized David's brothers, the other soldiers of the vast army, and even their God-chosen leader, King Saul. Everyone was intimidated and afraid of this audacious bully—and for good reason, based on his size and stature. David, however, refused to let fear interfere with his outraged determination.

> Now the Israelites had been saying, "Do you see how this man keeps coming out? He comes out to defy Israel. The king will give great wealth to the man who kills him. He will also give him his daughter in marriage and will exempt his family from taxes in Israel."
>
> David asked the men standing near him, "What will be done for the man who kills this Philistine and removes this disgrace from Israel? Who is this uncircumcised Philistine that he should defy the armies of the living God?"
>
> They repeated to him what they had been saying and told him, "This is what will be done for the man who kills him."
>
> When Eliab, David's oldest brother, heard him speaking with the men, he burned with anger at him and asked, "Why have you come down here? And with whom did you leave those few sheep in the wilderness? I know how conceited you are and how wicked your heart is; you came down only to watch the battle."

> "Now what have I done?" said David. "Can't I even speak?" He then turned away to someone else and brought up the same matter, and the men answered him as before. What David said was overheard and reported to Saul, and Saul sent for him.
>
> David said to Saul, "Let no one lose heart on account of this Philistine; your servant will go and fight him."
>
> Saul replied, "You are not able to go out against this Philistine and fight him; you are only a young man, and he has been a warrior from his youth."
>
> 1 Samuel 17:25–33

David immediately recognized that Goliath was not simply threatening the Israelite army—this braggart was assaulting their faith in the living God! As David saw it, not only was this pagan Philistine insulting his opponents—he was disrespecting their God. Something had to be done. And since no one else was willing, David stepped up. He was willing to take responsibility and face what everyone else was too afraid to face.

Being willing is all God asks of us.

Willing to face our fears.

Willing to take a stand.

Willing to rely on His power.

Willing to follow His lead.

Willing to do what no one else will do or can do.

Unexpected Resistance

Instead of receiving immediate support and encouragement, however, David had to confront a more familiar kind of bullying—from his brothers. Sibling rivalry nearly always emerges at some point in family dynamics, and it was no different with Jesse's eight sons. And I can't help but think David's older brothers already had a bigger chip on their shoulders because the prophet Samuel had passed them by and ended up anointing their kid brother instead. They probably thought of David as being so young and inexperienced that they wondered how God—or anyone, for that matter—could choose this rough-and-tumble teenaged shepherd to lead their entire nation. It was unthinkable—until it happened.

And now here was their kid brother, David, trying to butt in and act as though he could ever stand a chance against a renowned, enormous, muscle-bound, armor-clad giant like Goliath. Once again, it was madness to even consider! So much so that David's oldest brother, Eliab, "burned with anger" and questioned everything about David's motives for being there. Eliab implies David has neglected his duties as shepherd in order to come to the battlefront and be entertained by the spectacle. And why does big brother make this accusation? Because, he says, "I know how conceited you are and how wicked your heart is; you came down only to watch the battle" (1 Samuel 17:28).

Here is someone who has known David his entire life criticizing not only his motives but David's character. Rather than commending his younger brother's courage or passionate faith, Eliab condemns David as conceited—full of only himself—and wicked at heart. Sadly, this kind of response to our willingness to take a stand is still common today. Others, including those closest to us—parents, siblings, kids, coworkers, friends, and neighbors—will not necessarily support and encourage us to confront our giants. In fact, they may try to discourage, deflate, and dissuade us from doing what we know God is calling us to do.

As if the painful accusations of his brother weren't enough, David faced more unexpected resistance when his desire to take on Goliath was reported to the king—the same king who cowered in fear before the giant Philistine like everyone else. The same king who now scoffed at David's courageous and outrageous offer. Rather than commending David's bravery—after all, no one else had apparently volunteered to fight Goliath—Saul instead dismisses David.

Perhaps the king's reply was not as condescending and dismissive as it sounds to me today, but it's clear that in Saul's mind, there was no way David stood a chance. The logic is too overwhelmingly clear: David is an untested, inexperienced kid, and Goliath is an older, seasoned, battle-shrewd warrior. Which leads Saul to inform David, "You are not able to go out against this Philistine and fight him" (1 Samuel 17:33).

Perhaps Saul feels a moral duty to protect David from his own naivety and inexperienced ignorance.

But as you know, David could not be deterred.

His decision didn't require consideration. Goliath wasn't just a military enemy or tribal foe. Goliath had mocked and disrespected the living God. There was no way David could *not* stand up to such an affront! Because in that moment, David knew God had prepared him for the fight ahead.

> But David persisted. "I have been taking care of my father's sheep and goats," he said. "When a lion or a bear comes to steal a lamb from the flock, I go after it with a club and rescue the lamb from its mouth. If the animal turns on me, I catch it by the jaw and club it to death. I have done this to both lions and bears, and I'll do it to this pagan Philistine, too, for he has defied the armies of the living God! The LORD who rescued me from the claws of the lion and the bear will rescue me from this Philistine!"
>
> 1 Samuel 17:34–37 NLT

It wasn't bravado or conceit motivating David's willingness to face the Philistine giant. It was part of David's calling. He knew without a doubt that God had already been preparing him for that moment. David might have been only a boy-barely-a-man. He might have been a shepherd and not a soldier. He might have been the youngest and least experienced in battle. But David knew he was anointed!

God had chosen David as the next king of Israel and had been preparing him throughout his entire life. Because he was anointed by God, David knew he could not only confront Goliath but defeat this giant! When you are anointed, God always prepares you for the giants you must confront.

Giant Anointing

Our humility makes room for the anointing God has for us and allows us to see our battles from an eternal spiritual perspective, not the temporary skirmish we're facing in the moment. David knew there was much more at stake than just this battle for dominion over land. Goliath was challenging God's authority, God's character, and God's power. This giant was not taunting other soldiers—he was mocking faith in their God!

Despite not having support from his brothers or his king, David stepped up. While I hope you have a support system committed to your relationship with God and spiritual growth, and while I hope your primary relationships encourage you to face the towering giants in your life, you must realize that their support is supplemental and not essential. What is essential is your faith in God and His anointing on your life.

The psalmist declares, "I have been anointed with fresh oil" (Psalm 92:10 NKJV). While David is not explicitly credited for authorship, I suspect the shepherd king may have very well penned this divine declaration of his power source. When you are chosen by God and anointed for His purposes, just as Samuel anointed David, then your anointing empowers you to face anything life or the enemy throws at you. There is no giant that you cannot overcome through the power of God's Spirit in you!

Just like David, but upgraded exponentially through the finished work of Jesus Christ on the cross, you and I are anointed not to cower before bullies, not to run away from threats, not to assume we're losers, and not to be paralyzed by fear. We are not anointed with the power of God's Spirit to post more pics, go through the motions, perform for the applause of authors, or retreat into our private little bubble.

We are anointed with fresh oil to prove hell wrong!

From Genesis to Revelation through today, we discover the timeless truth of God's power in our lives. We experience power to overcome fear and to persevere. We realize we have been equipped for every battle before us. We have a giant anointing larger than any Goliath we face. When we are anointed, we are set apart for a holy purpose.

Anointed people do what others *will not do*.

Anointed people do what others *cannot do*.

Anointed people do not whine.

Anointed people worship.

Anointed people do not focus on the darkness.

Anointed people turn on the light.

Anointed people do not make excuses.

Anointed people make history.
Anointed people don't cower in fear.
Anointed people confront their giants!

Selecting Your Stone

As you consider the biblical truths and prophetic promises from this chapter, invite God's Spirit to guide and direct your understanding and application of them. Once again, don't allow these questions to become a burden or obligation. Instead, use them as an additional opportunity to draw closer to God as you explore the life of David and learn more about your own anointing from his experience. While you don't have to write down your responses, you will likely find it helpful both now to clarify your thoughts as well as later for further contemplation.

Regardless of how you engage with these questions, you're encouraged to spend a few minutes in prayer as you reflect and respond to this chapter. A brief prayer is provided to get you started, but make the words your own as you express the longings of your heart to know, love, and serve the Lord. Remember, His Spirit dwells in you and empowers you to face any and all giants looming in your life right now.

1. When have you encountered a bully in your life, and how did you respond? What influenced the way you responded as well as the result of this confrontation?

2. Who has doubted your ability to face the giants blocking your path forward? How have they tried to deter you from taking the stand you needed to take?

3. How are you currently standing firm in the face of opposition? How has God prepared and equipped you for this battle against those who mock Him?

Dear God, You know the giants I'm facing right now, the ongoing battles with persistent sinful habits and addictive cycles, the enemies who intend to harm me, the friends and family who seemingly try to undermine my ability to face my foes. During these showdowns, Lord, remind me of what's true, of what You have called me to do, of how You have equipped and prepared me for this moment. Let my confidence reside in You and in the limitless power of Your Spirit to do what is impossible in my own ability. May others see Your glory and goodness reflected in how I handle adversity and overcome obstacles. In Jesus' name, Amen.

3

Removing Saul's Armor

Shedding What Does Not Belong to You

You can't fight your giants with someone else's anointing. When you face the giants of your generation, your God-given anointing provides all the spiritual armor you need!

Armor is as old as human conflict.

When we think of armor today, it's usually the boxy metal medieval suits covering knights from head to toe that comes to mind. But armor in all kinds of varieties has been used to protect the human body for many centuries. From ancient times, warriors, soldiers, and combatants have tried to defend their bodies by using layers that were hardened or reinforced by wood, leather, stone, and metal. Logically enough, armor has typically protected the most vulnerable parts of the body—head, heart, internal organs, and limbs.

As civilizations progressed, improvements in armor advanced as well. Metal proved to be one of the best and most reliable materials, being both malleable and moldable when heated but then hard and dense when cooled. The only challenge, of course, was the added weight and decreased mobility. The thicker the armor, the heavier the added weight, which limited agility. Ideally, armor provided wearers with additional protection without impeding their ability to fight.

With advancements in military equipment and weaponry, armor was forced to evolve as well. While soldiers and law enforcement officers today don't wear bronze hoods and plated garments to shield their bodies, they still use body armor: combat helmets, night-vision goggles, and tactical vests made of Kevlar or ceramic alloys. Technology has also helped improve the defensive bodywear worn by various military, police, and security agents. Depending on the kind of tactical engagement, they may rely more on soft body armor than harder tactical gear.

The use of armor has also extended beyond the battlefield into other realms of rivalry and competition. Contact sports, such as American football, certainly come to mind with helmets, mouthguards, shoulder pads, and knee and shin guards mandatory at most levels of play. Baseball, hockey, and boxing similarly require protective gear for players in order to avoid injuries. Other sports, including motor sports and cycling, insist that participants wear helmets as well as heat- and fire-resistant clothing.

In addition to sports, armor has become a metaphor for any apparel used to protect oneself or assert an image of fierce confidence. Just consider the dapper suit worn by a successful attorney in the courtroom, the little black dress worn at society events, the colorful pants and polos worn on the golf course, and the edgy street wear favored by teens and young adults on social media. Many pastors have a certain look they wear when preaching as well. While I try to dress appropriately for the occasion, if I'm preaching in my home church, I tend to go for casually comfortable. My jeans, shirt, and blazer may not be suitable armor for combat, but they definitely work for spiritual warfare!

Clothes Make the Man

While I want to look "presentable," as my mother used to say, when I'm speaking or preaching or leading a meeting, I also want what I wear to reflect my style and personality. I can wear a suit when required, but I prefer clothes that are more relaxed and comfortable, what's now often called business casual. While we've all heard "clothes make the man," I learned early in my ministry that trying to look a certain way just because it was trendy or popular (and just because all my peers looked so cool wearing it) didn't work so well. I'll spare you the details of trying skinny jeans and bold chunky sweaters, but trust me—it wasn't pretty! Instead, often through trial and error, I discovered what was comfortable in fit and with a style that reflected who I was. Those are often the best kinds of uniforms—and also the best kinds of armor.

David discovered this truth the hard way. Once he agreed to confront the mighty Philistine warrior Goliath, a fight no other Hebrew soldier was willing to engage, David faced the pressure of strategic preparation. You will recall that David, outraged with righteous indignation over Goliath's disrespect for the God of Israel, stepped up to confront this frightening foe. And instead of being cheered and encouraged, David faced contempt from his brothers and condescension from his king. Undeterred and resolute in his mission, David insisted and explained, "The LORD who rescued me from the paw of the lion and the paw of the bear will rescue me from the hand of this Philistine" (1 Samuel 17:37).

Saul, the king who had dismissed David's youth and inexperience, accepted that the young shepherd could not be dissuaded. He finally consented, saying, "Go, and the LORD be with you" (1 Samuel 17:37). Apparently, the king who was too fearful to confront Goliath, offered what he himself could not use.

> Then Saul gave David his own armor—a bronze helmet and a coat of mail. David put it on, strapped the sword over it, and took a step or two to see what it was like, for he had never worn such things before.
>
> "I can't go in these," he protested to Saul. "I'm not used to them." So David took them off again. He picked up five smooth stones from a stream and put them into his shepherd's bag. Then, armed only with his shepherd's staff and sling, he started across the valley to fight the Philistine.
>
> 1 Samuel 17:38–40 NLT

Whether Saul wanted to protect the young military novice or assuage the guilt he felt for his own cowardice, or both—he doesn't express his motive. But doesn't it seem strange that one moment Saul is discounting David and saying he doesn't stand a chance against such an experienced warrior and then the next offering his personal armor? Why bother to offer something so significant to someone you don't believe in?

Those who don't support you in your fight forfeit the right to prepare you for battle.

Mixed Messages

This shift in Saul's attitude requires our consideration because there are people just like him still around today. Right away, Saul basically declared, "Hey, David—don't be *ridiculous*! Someone like you will *never* defeat Goliath. You don't have the first qualification to overtake a pro like him. There's no way you can fight this Philistine and possibly hope to win! You're only a boy, and he's been a triumphant man of war since his youth" (see 1 Samuel 17:33).

After David insists, Saul reluctantly gives his consent. He might as well since David is determined to confront the obnoxious giant. Saul then places his armor on David. Do you see the problem with this?

First, Saul tells David, "I don't believe in you," and only a few moments later he tells David, "Here, wear my armor." So which is it? One second David is a buffoon for daring to think he could face Goliath, and the next he's the king's proxy worthy of wearing the royal armor. There's more that doesn't fit here than an oversized metal suit.

Even if Saul's armor fit David like a glove and felt comfortable and natural to him, David still could not wear it. Because the giver of this supposed gift doesn't believe in what David is called to do. Mixed messages don't allow for miracles. The king seems more interested in saving face than supporting grace. Just imagine how embarrassing it was for Saul to have this country bumpkin show up and decide to fight this unbeatable adversary!

Saul, the king of Israel, could not muster the courage to confront this mouthy, brash opponent, but he was about to let this kid named David fight? Surely the least Saul could do was prolong the inevitable for a few minutes by encasing David in the finest, most ornate armor available. Later, he could tell his men, "I tried to warn that kid—even gave him my own armor."

David wasn't wearing someone else's armor—and neither should you.

Do not permit those who never believed in your calling, who have never embraced what God was doing in, with, and through you to place *anything* of theirs on you. Not their armor, their defensiveness, their fears, their cowardice, their insecurity, their guilt and shame—nothing!

Never wear the armor of a person who has never believed in you! Never put on the armor of the ones who dismiss you, belittle you, ignore you, or discount you. Don't receive from those who don't believe.

Like David, make it clear that you have been equipped supernaturally by the One who created you and called you into battle with this giant. Tell those unwilling, unable, and unavailable to fight or to support your fight, "If you don't believe I can do it, then I don't want your armor!"

I don't want your suggestions.

I don't want your advice.

I don't want your recommendations.

I don't want your input.

I don't want your strategy.

If you don't believe in what I'm called to do, then why should I rely on anything you provide? Like Saul attempting to prepare David for battle with Goliath, these people aren't concerned about *your fight*—they're covering up *their fright*. They want to feel as though they did what they could even as they predict that you cannot do what God has equipped and empowered you to do!

When you are anointed by God to overcome the giants of your generation, He will provide all you need for your battle.

Shed the Armor, Shine the Glory

Just as David was about to confront the giant no one else was willing to fight, he was surrounded by people who did not believe in him. His brothers did not believe in him. His big brother Eliab rebuked him as conceited and wicked. He was not his father's first choice. The king did not believe in him. But God's anointing on David was more than sufficient for him to overcome the giant.

David did not have to believe in himself because he believed in God. God had helped David in the past to protect his flocks against lions and bears. Keep in mind David had no shotguns, hunting rifles, or handguns—just a shepherd's staff and a slingshot. But God had infused this young shepherd with a fierce and courageous determination to kill those ferocious lions and bears before they could kill him or his sheep. Rather than run from them, David ran toward them! So now that he was about to face a man deadlier than any wild animal, David knew the Lord would strengthen him once again. David's self-confidence emerged from his utter confidence in God's Spirit.

There comes a time when it's just you and your anointing.

There comes a time when it's just you and the Holy Spirit.

There comes a time when it's just you and the name of Jesus.

There comes a time when it's just you and your Abba Father.

There comes a time when your security resides in the fact that the blood of Jesus washes you, covers you, and protects you.

There comes a time when God gets all the glory for empowering you to slay a giant.

Which brings up another good reason not to wear someone else's armor: You are called and anointed to remove the possibility of anyone else getting the glory instead of God! Don't allow anyone to use the association of their armor to take credit for what God has done in your life.

If we are following the logical continuum of the king's behavior, we can embrace the strong, almost certain possibility that the reason Saul wanted David to put on his armor and defeat Goliath is because Saul wanted the glory for the victory. Saul himself was too afraid to confront the giant Philistine, but perhaps the king thought he could save face by "allowing" David to wear the royal armor.

If David got decimated, which seemed likely based on the rationale of comparing size, strength, and experience, then Saul could shrug and say, "Well, I told him so. Tried to help by giving him my armor. Did all I could do." On the other hand, if by some divine miracle this rough-and-ready shepherd managed to slay this giant, then Saul could say, "Well done! I knew my armor would protect you and allow you to remain in the fight until you managed to defeat this warrior." So perhaps in some corner of Saul's mind, offering his armor to David was a self-directed attempt at finding a win-win in a situation that had up until that moment been lose-lose.

If this sounds overly critical of the king's motives, please consider that this was not an isolated incident. We know from Scripture that King Saul was what can best be described in twenty-first-century clinical terms as a narcissist: a self-absorbed, self-inflated, and self-seeking individual. Narcissists love power so that they can be the center of their universe, directing others to serve them, compliment them, obey them.

And not only did Saul focus on himself more than others—he focused on himself more than God! Saul's disobedience resulted in God declaring, "'I regret that I have made Saul king, because he has turned away from me and has not carried out my instructions.' Samuel was angry, and he cried out to the LORD all that night" (1 Samuel 15:11).

Offering his armor wasn't just Saul being generous. It wasn't just about, "Here, David, use my stuff." It was more likely, "Here, David, use my stuff so that if you defeat the giant, the people will say that you defeated the giant because you were using my stuff."

Shed the armor of others so that only God's glory shines through!

Thanks, but No Thanks

Plenty of King Sauls still exist in our world, and you have likely encountered some of them. These are the people who want to place their stuff on you when they say it is for your good in order for them to get the glory. Sometimes it's not their armor but their advice. They make excuses for why they can't fight this battle but suddenly believe they can tell you how to do it. Or it might be their fears and insecurities they heap on you in order to prop up their own fragile, frightened egos. They employ their stealthy, passive-aggressive style of communication and say, "I'm not able to win this battle, but if you think you can, then be my guest. Just keep in mind that no one expects you to win, okay? But we admire your courage and willingness to try."

The Sauls of this world often see one way to victory over the giants of their generation—their way. Saul assumed that in order for David to defeat Goliath, David must be equipped as Saul would have been equipped—with the same helmet, chain mail, and sword. But when David tried it on, he realized that what was supposed to help him was actually a liability. He felt like a kid playing dress-up, tripping over himself and awkwardly trying to use a weapon that was not his own.

David's response to King Saul required just as much faith as confronting Goliath.

It took courage to tell his king, "Thanks—but no thanks. That might work for you, but it doesn't work for me. I've already been anointed. God has already prepared me for this fight. I have everything I need."

There comes a time when God will compel you to do the same, a time when He will say to you, "Don't put on anyone else's stuff because I'm going to see you through. Don't be afraid to refuse what others insist on giving you. You have everything you need already—I promise."

Have you been wearing someone else's armor in order to battle the giants in your life? Perhaps the armor is from your friends and family, your pastor, your AA sponsor, your counselor, your prayer partner, your mentor, your Bible study leader, your spouse—and perhaps they mean well when they tell you what you need to do to win your war. But somehow it doesn't feel right. You wonder if you're doing what they've instructed just to please them rather than to slay your giant. You realize that trying to win the battle their way is simply not working.

We often overlook that God anoints us and equips us to slay our giants.

You have a choice: either someone else's armor or God's anointing.

Anointing or Armor?

So which will it be? Someone else's armor, or God's anointing?

Which one will advance you to your place of divine destiny?

Which one will empower you to bring down the giants?

Which one will enable you to occupy your Jerusalem and bring the glory of God into your destiny?

It's time to shed the weight of others' armor in your life.

It's time to shrug off the advice, labels, and expectations from others that you've been wearing. Get ready to lighten your load and experience the agility and mobility God has instilled in you. Today is the day the cumbersome, clunky, ill-fitting armor is coming off your life. Today is the day the false armor is coming off your family, your inheritance, and your generation.

Why? Because you don't need anyone else's armor when you have the armor of God!

When you've experienced the anointing of God's Spirit in your life, you have spiritual armor that provides both defensive and offensive covering better than any suit of metal. In his letter to the believers in Ephesus, Paul describes the invisible, supernatural armor we've been given.

> Put on all of God's armor so that you will be able to stand firm against all strategies of the devil. For we are not fighting against flesh-and-blood enemies, but against evil rulers and authorities of the unseen world, against mighty powers in this dark world, and against evil spirits in the heavenly places.
>
> Therefore, put on every piece of God's armor so you will be able to resist the enemy in the time of evil. Then after the battle you will still be standing firm. Stand your ground, putting on the belt of truth and the body armor of God's righteousness. For shoes, put on the peace that comes from the Good News so that you will be fully prepared. In addition to all of these, hold up the shield of faith to stop the fiery arrows of the devil. Put on salvation as your helmet, and take the sword of the Spirit, which is the word of God.
>
> Pray in the Spirit at all times and on every occasion. Stay alert and be persistent in your prayers for all believers everywhere.
>
> Ephesians 6:11–18 NLT

Saul's armor was undoubtedly custom-made by the finest metalsmith available in Israel. It was not only made of the finest metal, probably bronze, but likely decorated with embellishments fit for a king. This royal armor had likely been battle-tested, if not by Saul himself then by soldiers proving its effectiveness to make sure it was worthy of their leader.

David rejected this armor and instead went with what he already had: "I cannot go in these . . . because I am not used to them," he told the king (1 Samuel 17:39). And after taking off Saul's armor, David went with what he had always relied on. "He picked up five smooth stones from a stream and put them into his shepherd's bag. Then, armed only with his shepherd's staff and sling, he started across the valley to fight the Philistine" (1 Samuel 17:40 NLT).

As you know, it only took one stone expertly placed to fell the giant.

Just one stone.

Because David relied on what he already had.

Do you know what you already have?

If you have accepted the free gift of salvation through Jesus, then you have been anointed by God with another gift, the Holy Spirit dwelling in you. With the anointing of the Spirit, you have continual 24/7 access to the spiritual armor of God. Through your anointing, you are wearing:

The Belt of Truth. Because when you know the truth, "the truth will set you free" (John 8:32).

The Body Armor of God's Righteousness. "If you know that he is righteous, you know that everyone who does what is right has been born of him" (1 John 2:29).

Shoes of Peace that come from our security in the Good News. "Peace I leave with you; my peace I give you. I do not give to you as the world gives. Do not let your hearts be troubled and do not be afraid" (John 14:27).

The Shield of Faith. "For God has not given us a spirit of fear and timidity, but of power, love, and self-discipline" (2 Timothy 1:7 NLT).

The Helmet of Salvation. "For I am not ashamed of the gospel, because it is the power of God that brings salvation to everyone who believes" (Romans 1:16).

The Sword of the Spirit, the Word of God. "For the word of God is alive and active. Sharper than any double-edged sword, it penetrates even to dividing soul and spirit, joints and marrow; it judges the thoughts and attitudes of the heart" (Hebrews 4:12).

You are more than equipped to slay any and all giants before you. Goliath never wins—*never*!

Why? Because nothing compares to the spiritual armor of God!

Let Your Faith Fit

David was called.

David was anointed.

David was equipped.

David was able to slay a giant no one else would confront. And yet, in order for him to defeat the giant of his generation, David had to shed Saul's armor. He could not pretend to feel comfortable in someone else's protection. He had never worn armor like this before, so why should he attempt to wear it now—in the biggest fight of his life? I suspect David knew Saul's armor was not a fit for him before he even put it on.

In order for David, empowered by the Spirit of the almighty God, to accomplish his first humanly impossible mission, David had to shed Saul's armor.

Just like David—and even to a greater degree through the finished work of Jesus Christ—you are called to do the same, to learn from David's example and let go of what others place on you, project onto you, and heap on you.

Just like David and with a greater dimension, through the indwelling of the Holy Spirit, you are anointed. And yet you can be both called and anointed and unable to defeat the giant in your family and your generation if you are wearing someone else's armor. It's time to let your faith fit the battle you're facing.

Too many Christians, too many people in the Church, find themselves unable to overcome the giants in front of them because they are wearing someone else's armor.

You can't fight your giant with someone else's anointing.

You can't get your breakthrough with someone else's praise.

You cannot fulfill your purpose with someone else's promise.

You cannot live out your destiny with someone else's identity.

You have to wear your own armor.

You have to carry your own testimony.

God's Word tells us that we overcome by the blood of the Lamb and the word of our testimony (see Revelation 12:11).

God's Word tells us that we have spiritual armor to fight battles against the unseen forces of the enemy (see Ephesians 6:11–18).

God's Word tells us that we can do all things through Christ who strengthens us (see Philippians 4:13).

Stop trying to make other people's armor fit.

Start living in the fullness of all you have been given in the Spirit.

You are called and anointed, and that is enough!

Selecting Your Stone

By now you know the following questions are provided to enhance your understanding of this chapter and to help you process and apply the truths shared here. As you read through them slowly and thoughtfully, allow the Holy Spirit to clarify what you've been wearing and carrying that does not belong to you. Consider where you have been allowing other people, past events, or your own false assumptions to come between you and your unique identity in Christ.

Once again, the brief prayer below is intended to start your conversation —not be a substitute for it—with God about all you're learning and experiencing right now. Take a deep breath and still your heart before Him, listening to the voice of the Spirit and the truth of His Word that comes to mind. Ask Him to help you remove any unnecessary armor you've been wearing and to trust how He has equipped you for the battles you face. Remember, your anointing is more powerful than any armor!

1. When have others tried to help encourage, prepare, or equip you for a battle you ultimately needed to fight alone? How did you respond to the "armor" they offered?

2. What are some of the unique ways God has equipped you and prepared you for where you are in your life right now? What past experiences have revealed God's hand at work in your life presently?

3. Why do you sometimes struggle to refuse the armor offered by others and to trust that God has equipped you with His spiritual armor right where you are? What do you need to release in order to travel lighter in the power of the Spirit?

Dear Lord, You know how I have sometimes tried to please others in the past. You understand those times when I've tried to be cooperative and collaborative, often trying to meet others' expectations rather than trusting in how You have equipped me. Remind me of the many ways You have sustained me and prepared me for the battles I'm facing. Give me the strength and courage not only for the giants I face but for the ways others attempt to help me in the process. I know that You have anointed me for great things, and I love discovering more of the divine purpose You've chosen me to fulfill. In Jesus' name, Amen.

SECOND STONE

INTIMACY

Anointed to Slay Your Giants with Authority

I have given you authority to trample on snakes and scorpions and to overcome all the power of the enemy; nothing will harm you.

Luke 10:19

4

Anointed from the Inside Out

Experiencing God's Spirit in You

> You have been anointed by an intimate encounter with the Spirit of God. Your anointing gives you authority to overcome anything the enemy throws at you!

While I confess that I'm not much of a camper, I love the incredible beauty of God's creative imagination displayed in the natural world. Folsom Lake is one such spot about twenty-five miles northeast of Sacramento. A popular state recreation area and one of the most visited state parks in California, Folsom Lake is actually a reservoir formed by the Folsom Dam, which was built in 1955 to manage and direct the American River. The last time I visited this beautiful waterway, I was privileged to watch the sun descend to the lake's horizon shortly before a storm blew in. The contrast between the crimson ball burning gold atop Folsom's horizontal deep blue water thrilled me, but another contrast made an even greater impression that evening.

The lake water reflected the sunlight in a way that illuminated its calm, placid surface. There was a stillness, as if the natural world had temporarily held its breath, pausing just as I had to take in the stunning sunset. Nothing moved, only the light shimmering on a flat azure plane of still water. It was eerily quiet, the proverbial calm before the storm.

Then just as the sun sank deeper behind the horizon leaving pink and orange streaks, suddenly a massive wind seemed to come out of nowhere. From right to left, the lake's surface undulated into small crescents like tiny sails catching the wind, like liquid dominoes toppling across the entire expanse, stirring up a choppy foam that had been smooth as glass only moments previously. Trees shuddered in the distance with their branches rocking and leaves fluttering. Clouds seemed to descend out of nowhere. Small waves rippled toward me, and I felt the wind on shore as well, cooling my face and arms with a brisk ferocity. Refreshing but also strong enough to command respect for its unseen power and the way it heralded a shift in the weather.

In that moment, I witnessed one of the best illustrations of the Holy Spirit I have ever encountered. Specifically, I was reminded of creation, of God's Spirit looming above the expanse of dark nothingness before He spoke and creation began. "Now the earth was formless and empty, darkness was over the surface of the deep, and the Spirit of God was hovering over the waters" (Genesis 1:2). The Hebrew word here for Spirit is *ruach*, which literally refers to "a violent exhalation, a blast of breath, a strong wind."

Like the sunset calm before the storm blew in over Folsom Lake, an invisible force of air burst across a vast stillness resulting in dynamic motion. The Spirit of God was there hovering, in the empty, shapeless void one moment before this powerful breath of wind initiated the formation of the earth, light and dark, land and water, and all the living creatures on land and sea. It's as if this divine supernatural breath infused energy into all forms of life in this new intricate creation.

Trash Talk and Idol Threats

In addition to the Spirit being the divine catalyst for creation, I was also reminded that evening at Folsom Lake of the moments in between when David selected his five stones and when he sent one of them into the forehead of Goliath. Perhaps it's just my notion of the calm before the storm, but I imagine the scene of their imminent confrontation to be charged with tension and the urgent sense that something powerful was about to happen. After all, David had just returned the king's armor to Saul and chosen to go with an unprecedented strategy of his own, a battle plan based not on equipment but on being equipped by God.

While the two armies likely went silent and held their collective breath, the two adversaries approached one another and traded what we today often call "trash talk." The strategy behind trash talk seems to be that you get inside your opponent's mind and cause them to doubt themselves. You try to play on their insecurities and perceived weaknesses, perhaps insulting their appearance, their size, their weaponry, or their underlying fear. Embedded in the trash talk exchanged between David and Goliath, however, is something much more important—divine authority.

> Goliath walked out toward David with his shield bearer ahead of him, sneering in contempt at this ruddy-faced boy. "Am I a dog," he roared at David, "that you come at me with a stick?" And he cursed David by the names of his gods. "Come over here, and I'll give your flesh to the birds and wild animals!" Goliath yelled.
>
> 1 Samuel 17:41–44 NLT

Notice the way Goliath, for all his bragging and arrogant self-confidence, nonetheless allows his shield bearer to precede him, to come between him and this upstart foolish enough to challenge him. No surprise either that the Philistine sneered in contempt, and seeing David's shepherd's staff, compared it to a stick used to fend off a wild dog. I love the irony in Goliath's challenge because basically he accuses David of disrespecting and underestimating him—when, in fact, it's Goliath who vastly underestimates this inexperienced young man on a mission.

Most striking of all, however, is the fact that Goliath "cursed David by the names of his gods" (1 Samuel 17:43) before threatening to feed David's carcass to the birds and beasts. While the pagan Philistines likely idolized a number of gods, three specific ones are mentioned elsewhere in the Old Testament: Dagon, god of grains and agriculture

(Judges 16:23, 1 Samuel 5); Ashtoreth, also known as Astarte, goddess of fertility, love, and war (1 Samuel 31:10); and Baal-Zebub, literally meaning "lord of the flies," the god of prophecy and destruction (2 Kings 1:2–3).[1] Goliath uses the names of these gods as a way of invoking authority. Suddenly, David's willingness to stand up to the giant is about more than military dominion—it's about beliefs, culture, and religion.

To his credit, David apparently wasn't frightened by these threats. If anything, the curses and shade thrown by Goliath only served to get David more fired up. And in stark contrast to calling upon his God to curse the Philistine, David made it clear that everything he was doing and everything that was about to happen was due to the power of the living God and for His glory.

> David replied to the Philistine, "You come to me with sword, spear, and javelin, but I come to you in the name of the LORD of Heaven's Armies—the God of the armies of Israel, whom you have defied. Today the LORD will conquer you, and I will kill you and cut off your head. And then I will give the dead bodies of your men to the birds and wild animals, and the whole world will know that there is a God in Israel! And everyone assembled here will know that the LORD rescues his people, but not with sword and spear. This is the LORD's battle, and he will give you to us!"
>
> 1 Samuel 17:45–47 NLT

With these prophetic words, David reduced this showdown to the basis of power for each side. While Goliath relied on his shield bearer, his sword, spear, and javelin, David emphasized the only thing he had, the only thing required for this battle. "I come to you in the name of the LORD of Heaven's Armies—the God of the armies of Israel, whom you have defied."

David has been anointed.

David has the power of the Spirit of God.

David has the authority of the Lord God Almighty.

1. *Bible Hub Topical Encyclopedia*, "Gods of the Philistines," accessed February 27, 2026, https://biblehub.com/topical/g/gods_of_the_philistines.htm.

On Good Authority

How do I know this? Because the same word used for God's Spirit in Genesis and throughout the Old Testament, *ruach*, is used when David is anointed by God's prophet Samuel. "So Samuel took the horn of oil and anointed him in the presence of his brothers, and from that day on the Spirit of the LORD came powerfully upon David" (1 Samuel 16:13). Like entering a wind tunnel, from that moment until the end of his life, David experienced the ongoing, sustaining, life-giving power of God's Spirit in his life. While this anointing empowered David for all the challenges he would face, including the giant he would soon slay, the Spirit of the Lord upon David also gave him authority—specifically, God's authority.

Perhaps you've heard the figure of speech "on good authority." It's often used to reinforce the credibility and reliability of an unnamed source, someone who might not want to go on record and be named for whatever reason but who has firsthand knowledge, insight, or expertise that they are willing to share. Ultimately, though, authority is only as good as the identity, character, and power of its source. Unnamed and unknown sources may or may not be trustworthy since we don't know their name, their integrity, or their strength.

Calling on the authority of God's name, however, is not merely good authority—it's the best authority! The authority of God supersedes all other authority on heaven and earth. He is the brilliant Creator, the Holy of Holies, Jehovah Jireh, our heavenly Father. He is both the first and last word, the Alpha and Omega, the Word made flesh, the ultimate and supreme authority with limitless power and incomparable goodness and unconditional love for His children.

Because we have been anointed by His Spirit, we have supernatural authority.

We see throughout the pages of Scripture that calling on the name of God, on the name of Jesus Christ, carries supernatural authority. After His resurrection, Jesus proclaimed to His disciples:

> All authority in heaven and on earth has been given to me. Therefore go and make disciples of all nations, baptizing them in the name of the Father and of the Son and of the Holy Spirit, and teaching them to obey

> everything I have commanded you. And surely I am with you always, to the very end of the age.
>
> Matthew 28:18–20

God the Father granted all authority to His Son who, with His death and resurrection, gives the gift of the Holy Spirit to those who believe—forever.

Throughout Christ's ministry on earth, we see Him dispensing His divine authority to His followers in order to overcome the enemy and restore wholeness. "When Jesus had called the Twelve together, he gave them power and authority to drive out all demons and to cure diseases, and he sent them out to proclaim the kingdom of God and to heal the sick" (Luke 9:1–2). Notice Jesus gave them not only power but also His authority, the basis for His divine power as the Son of God, in order to dispel evil and to cure diseases, to share the Good News of the Gospel message and to heal those who were unwell.

David had authority on behalf of the Lord and because of God's Spirit dwelling in him to defy seemingly impossible odds and topple a giant. David could not sit idly by and refused to cower in fear because this enemy had done the unthinkable and unallowable—defied and defiled the name of the living God.

And the results likely shocked everyone there watching except for the young shepherd, chosen by God and anointed with His Spirit:

> As Goliath moved closer to attack, David quickly ran out to meet him. Reaching into his shepherd's bag and taking out a stone, he hurled it with his sling and hit the Philistine in the forehead. The stone sank in, and Goliath stumbled and fell face down on the ground.
>
> 1 Samuel 17:48–49 NLT

When God authorizes you with His anointing, *nothing is impossible*!

Authority of Your Anointing

The same divine authority that permitted David to defeat Goliath is available to you and me. When you are first anointed by the Spirit of

God, you become not only a beloved son or daughter, not only a co-heir with Christ, but an authorized ambassador for the Kingdom who seeks to reflect God's glory and draw others to Him as you follow the example of His Son. Your mission is simply to love and share the Good News of salvation through Jesus Christ. This divine authority enables you to overcome the evil one and to bless, heal, cure, protect, and provide for others in ways that defy human, rational, and logical understanding.

You have the living breath of God in you, which comes with divine authority.

Anointed with the divine authority and power of the Holy Spirit, you cannot be stopped!

Once again, don't take my word for it—take God's Word for it. In the New Testament, another word similar to *ruach* is used to refer to the Holy Spirit—*pneuma*. This Greek word also refers to a strong current of air, a powerful wind, a forceful breath. There is a sense of God infusing us with new life by breathing His Spirit into us. In fact, Jesus said, "The Spirit gives life. . . . The words I have spoken to you—they are full of the Spirit and life" (John 6:63).

Like a forceful, focused breath of fresh air, the Spirit refreshes and revives, renews and revitalizes us. We were once dead and stagnant in our sinful state, and when we accepted God's grace into our lives, we experienced a kind of holy CPR. Anointed by the power of God's Spirit, we receive new life, empowering us with divine authority to create, heal, resurrect, and overcome.

Adding up the number of times *ruach* and *pneuma* are used in the Bible, we see that the Spirit of God is referenced more than eight hundred times. While the Holy Spirit is described in other ways—as the Comforter, the Paraclete, our Advocate, Counselor, and Helper, this third person of the Godhead is most often expressed in language referencing breath and wind. This is certainly the case in one of the most vivid depictions when the gift of the Holy Spirit descended on the believers at Pentecost.

> When the day of Pentecost came, they were all together in one place. Suddenly a sound like the blowing of a violent wind came from heaven and filled the whole house where they were sitting. They saw what seemed to be tongues of fire that separated and came to rest on each of them.

> All of them were filled with the Holy Spirit and began to speak in other tongues as the Spirit enabled them.
>
> Acts 2:1–4

This mighty pneuma wind at Pentecost not only blew the Spirit of God into the hearts of those believers but opened the way to God's Spirit dwelling in *every* believer. You need to realize that Pentecost ushered in a new way of living and relating to God. Jesus did what no human being could ever do—He paid the debt for our sin and defeated death once and for all. As the Son of God, He had the Father's supernatural power and authority to accomplish these divine feats. But what's more than interesting, my friend, is how Scripture describes the source of Jesus' resurrection power. "The Spirit of God, who raised Jesus from the dead, lives in you" (Romans 8:11 NLT). The Spirit raised Jesus from the dead. Jesus overcame death and ascended to heaven. He sent the gift of His Spirit to live in you.

This is the authority of your anointing.
This is the authority of your healing.
This is the authority of your salvation.
This is the authority of your living as a new creature in Christ.
This is the authority of your relationship to the living God.
This is the authority of your triumph over the enemy.
This is the authority of your joy, your peace, your purpose.
This is the authority of your abundant life.
This is the authority of your restoration.
This is the authority of your redemption.

Royal Authority

By the authority of God's Word, you have divine resurrection power within you at this very moment. When Paul wrote to the followers of Jesus in Rome, he wanted to make sure they realized their direct and ongoing connection with God. They were not simply following the laws of God the Father as described by previous generations in the Old Testament. They were not simply following the example set by God's Son, Jesus, during His thirty-three years on earth. Paul wanted these

Christians to realize the divine overlap—the same Spirit who raised Jesus from the tomb was alive in them!

Living in the anointing of God's Spirit unconditionally was a radical shift in how people related to God. While God had chosen the people whom He anointed with His Spirit previously, like He did with David, with the work of the cross completed by Jesus, now everyone had access to the gift of God's Spirit. Paul wanted to make sure other believers grasped this new paradigm.

Now that these new followers of Jesus had been anointed with the Holy Spirit, Paul wanted to emphasize the changes within them and the manifestations beyond them. He wanted to help them realize what had already occurred within them so that they could shift from their previous ways of thinking, speaking, and behaving to their new Spirit-based way of living. They no longer had to try harder—they simply needed to rely on the Spirit of God within them.

This anointing in the Spirit is not simply a one-and-done historical event—the Holy Spirit is the living gift that keeps on giving! Because the same Spirit that defeated death and resurrected the cold body of Jesus lying dead in the borrowed tomb sealed by an enormous boulder, the same Spirit that activated resurrection of Christ's body—this Spirit is the same One who resides in you.

If the Spirit of God, who raised Jesus from the dead, lives in you, then you can overcome death.

If the Spirit of God, who anointed David as king of Israel, empowered and authorized him to slay a giant, then you can slay the giants of your generation.

If the Spirit of God, who hovered over an empty, dark void and created into existence what had never been before, then you can create into existence something that was not there before you.

With the same Spirit, David was anointed with royal authority.

Others—his own father and brothers—overlooked him, but God did not look at external appearances. He instead looked at David's heart. And what He saw was a man after God's own heart, someone willing to receive an anointing of God's Spirit and all the power and authority that came with such a gift.

David's life was never the same after this anointing. The Spirit of the Lord came upon David in power. The Spirit of the Lord granted David authority to call on the name of the Lord, and the Spirit of the Lord equipped David to defeat giants.

The same Spirit of the Lord continues to anoint you!

Despite those who have refused to believe in you.

Despite the presence of those who have criticized you.

Despite the condescension of those who have dismissed you.

Despite the armor heaped on you by those around you.

Despite the size of the giant looming in front of you.

Despite the curses, threats, and intimidation of others.

The same Spirit of the Lord has anointed you from the inside out.

Eternally Updated Edition

The challenge with living in the authority of your anointing often emerges in your thinking, in the narrative that is no longer accurate but that you continue to tell yourself. This is why Paul spotlighted the significance of realizing the same Spirit is in us—guiding, comforting, advising, holding, loving, befriending, empowering, equipping—that raised the Son of God from the grave. When the Spirit of God anoints you, your story takes the ultimate divine twist.

You are no longer trapped in the past, in old wounds, in previous mistakes, in prior struggles. You have the authority to claim the new story God is writing in your life. You simply have to stop repeating the default script and experience the fresh breath, the cleansing wind, the holy breeze of God's Spirit. Let Him turn the page in your life instead of going over the same chapter again and again.

Like Joseph, you're no longer in the pit—you're living your dream.

Like Moses, you're no longer in Egypt—you're parting the waters.

Like Joshua, you're no longer in the desert—you're in the Promised Land.

Like Ruth and Naomi, you're no longer grieving in Moab—you're starting over.

Like Shadrach, Meshach, and Abednego, you're not in the furnace—you're fireproof.

Like Lazarus, you're no longer in the tomb—you're removing your shroud.

Like Paul and Silas, you're no longer imprisoned—you're living in freedom.

No matter what story you've been living—God has authorized a new edition.

A newly revised and eternally updated edition!

You are no longer in darkness.

You are no longer in addiction.

You are no longer in failure.

You are no longer in shame.

You are no longer in religious condemnation.

You are no longer in past trauma.

You are no longer in present paralysis.

You are no longer in fear of the future.

You are alive in Jesus Christ through the power of the Holy Spirit!

You are no longer in what used to be.

Your old story no longer binds you.

You don't live there anymore.

You don't think there anymore.

You don't look there anymore.

You don't pray there anymore.

You don't search there anymore.

You don't sleep there anymore.

You don't shop there anymore.

You don't sow there anymore.

You are living in a new story authored by the ultimate Author and Authority!

The same Spirit that raised Jesus has raised, is raising, and will continue raising you.

The same Spirit that empowered and equipped David to defeat Goliath will continue empowering and equipping you to defeat any and all giants standing in your path.

The same Spirit that started creation has started a new creation in you!

Selecting Your Stone

Use the following questions to enhance your understanding and application of this chapter's revelations about the internal reality and external manifestation of your anointing. Consider this an opportunity to still yourself before God and receive a fresh breath of the Holy Spirit's life-giving power in your life. No matter where you are or what your circumstances, you have the resurrection power of God's Spirit within you.

So take a deep breath, clear your mind, and calm your heart as you invite the gentle, loving presence of the Spirit to comfort and guide you. Share any struggles or challenges you have been facing and be reminded of the authority you have over temptations and snares of the enemy. Ask the Holy Spirit to instill in you a new awareness of what it means to live in the fullness of your anointing: *You are chosen by God, filled with His Spirit, and anointed to prove hell wrong!*

1. When have you most recently experienced an intimate awareness of God's Spirit at work in you? What evidence did you (and others) see as a result of the Spirit's power in your life in this encounter?

2. What illustration, metaphor, or comparison best describes your experience of the Holy Spirit's presence in your life? Is it more like a breath of fresh air or a mighty wind—or something else?

3. Calling on the authority you have by the power of God's Spirit in you, what new story is God creating on the pages of your

life? What old narrative do you need to stop believing in order to fully inhabit your new story in Christ?

Dear God, thank You for giving me a fresh encounter with the gift of Your Holy Spirit in my life. I praise and worship You for allowing me to know You and experience Your presence in such an intimate relationship. You have changed the story of my life, and I remain forever grateful. Guide and direct me, Lord, as I deflect the assaults of the enemy and overcome all obstacles in my path. Let me live from the inside out and manifest Your authority and power in all that I do, and all for Your glory. May the story of my life reflect Your glory in all that I do. In Jesus' name, Amen.

5

More Than One Stone

Equipped to Slay Every Giant You Face

You can live in the confidence of your anointing and know you have more than one stone. You have all you need to defeat today's giant—and all future giants!

"Don't bring a knife to a gunfight."

You've probably heard this idiom before, either in casual conversation or in movies and TV shows. Allegedly, the saying originated in the Wild West during the late nineteenth century in the United States, which seems logical given the use of handguns and holsters associated with cowboys and lawmen of the period.[1] During a time when disputes and personal grievances were often settled with a duel or a shootout, a person would want to be armed with the right weapon. While knives had often been used on the frontier, they were no match for the speed and deadly force of a pistol, revolver, six-shooter, shotgun, or rifle.

Since then, the phrase has become a figurative way to describe a situation in which someone shows up unprepared, ill-equipped, or unaware

1. *LanGeek English*, "to bring a knife to a gunfight," accessed February 27, 2026, https://dictionary.langeek.co/en/word/219199.

of what they're facing. Not long ago, I was in a production meeting in Los Angeles to discuss the possibility of several new film projects. One of the presenters had prepared a slideshow to convey an overview of the movie idea he was pitching. While he did a fine job, the next presenter revealed his project by showing a six-minute video pitch, virtually a trailer for the film the team hoped to make. Another producer in that meeting whispered to me, "Looks like the first presenter brought a knife to a gunfight." His point was that comparatively the first pitch seemed basic and old-fashioned next to the flashy video shown after it.

His use of this figure of speech reminded me of one of my favorite films—*Raiders of the Lost Ark*—and a scene that's now become iconic. If you've seen the movie, then you know immediately the cinematic showdown I'm talking about. Set in the 1930s during the early days of World War II, the intrepid archaeologist Indiana Jones, played by Harrison Ford, must beat the Nazi in finding the remains of the Ark of the Covenant. The chase leads Indy to Cairo, where he's cornered in the outdoor marketplace by an unnamed, black-clad, sword-wielding assassin, played by professional stunt actor Terry Richards.

Steven Spielberg, the film's director, had storyboarded most of the movie prior to filming, particularly the numerous action sequences. Spielberg had originally intended this fight scene between Ford and Richards to be quite involved and choreographed, incorporating Indy's reliance on his trusty whip against the Arab assassin's scimitar. Anticipating this intense action scene, which would likely require two or three days in front of the cameras, Richards spent weeks mastering his sword skills—only to be sorely disappointed when it came time to film.

Shooting in Tunisia to depict Egypt, Spielberg and company faced unexpected circumstances that forced them to change the scene. A weeks-long heat wave with temperatures hovering well above one hundred degrees Fahrenheit made conditions stifling for everyone involved. To make matters worse, nearly all of the cast and crew were suffering from dysentery—including Harrison Ford. Due to heat and illness, production began running over budget. Instead of a long-drawn-out sword fight, Indy reaches for his gun in his side-holster, aims, and unexpectedly shoots his would-be assailant.[2]

Viewers enjoyed the unexpected anticlimactic moment and its vivid illustration of the old adage about the inadequacy of a knife—no matter how large—in a gunfight. Both the saying and this memorable scene remind us that the victor in most battles is usually determined by who has the best weapons and resources. But as David proved in slaying Goliath, sometimes you don't need a gun or a knife to win the fight.

You only need one smooth stone.

Run Toward Your Giant

David didn't bring a knife to a gunfight—he brought a slingshot to battle a sword, spear, and javelin. He brought more, of course, much more through the anointing authority and power of God's Spirit. David framed this battle as one between earthly weapons—Goliath's arsenal of assorted battle gear—and heavenly weapons. "You come to me with sword, spear, and javelin, but I come to you in the name of the LORD of Heaven's Armies—the God of the armies of Israel, whom you have defied" (1 Samuel 17:45 NLT).

Undaunted by David's invocation of Israel's God, the giant eagerly advanced. Goliath had likely grown restless of so much talk and so little action. Keep in mind, the Philistine warrior had been taunting the armies and king of Israel for forty days when David arrived on the scene (see 1 Samuel 17:16). Not one of Saul's soldiers dared to reply to Goliath, let alone accept his winner-take-all challenge. Instead, the Israelites cowered in fear and ran from the battlefront where the giant had taken his stand. And even after David had accepted the challenge and boldly determined to fight the giant, Goliath had to think that it would be no fight at all. He probably couldn't wait to decimate the obnoxious shepherd boy who shouted his faith-based bravado. Add in the smack talk they had exchanged, and Goliath was raring to go.

2. Federico Furzan, "Indiana Jones and the Weird Story Behind the Sword vs. Gun Scene," MovieWeb, December 9, 2023, https://movieweb.com/indiana-jones-true-story-sword-vs-gun-scene.

And this battle was indeed over before it began—but not as this giant expected!

> As Goliath moved closer to attack, David quickly ran out to meet him. Reaching into his shepherd's bag and taking out a stone, he hurled it with his sling and hit the Philistine in the forehead. The stone sank in, and Goliath stumbled and fell face down on the ground.
>
> So David triumphed over the Philistine with only a sling and a stone, for he had no sword. Then David ran over and pulled Goliath's sword from its sheath. David used it to kill him and cut off his head.
>
> 1 Samuel 17:48–51 NLT

Notice that as Goliath rushed to attack, David didn't wait around—he ran to meet his enemy! David's confidence was in the Lord and in his awareness of the anointing he had received, the anointing in which the Spirit of the Lord came upon him with power. David's confidence was in knowing that he did not need the king's armor—he had defeated lions and bears with only his simple shepherd's staff and slingshot. David's confidence was in the five stones he had selected only moments earlier from the nearby stream. In a battle filled with many surprises, the fact that David, this inexperienced underdog from Bethlehem, was more eager to fight than his overconfident opponent stands out.

David's example reminds us that we can run toward our Goliath when our confidence is in the Lord. I suspect that frequently we run *away* from the giants coming for us instead of running *toward* them. Our human bodies and brains are wired for survival, so when we encounter danger, our default responses are usually fight or flight, freeze or fawn. But David had enough time—and more than enough faith—to counter any human hesitation and charge into this battle.

So if you tend to feel paralyzed by fear when confronting your addiction, your job termination, your conviction, your injury, your illness, your bankruptcy, your abuse, your trauma, your betrayals—it's more than okay. It's simply *human*. Which is why in order to run into battle you need a response that's more than human, a response that's *supernatural*. A response that's spiritual instead of physical, that's based on the authority of your anointing instead of the authority of your government, that's confident in the power of God and not the strength of your body.

When you have been anointed by the Holy Spirit, you run toward your giant.

When you have been anointed by the Holy Spirit, you run into the fire.

When you have been anointed by the Holy Spirit, you can't wait to fight.

Why? Because God has equipped you especially for your battle.

No Sword Necessary

After a standoff that had lasted at least forty days, the actual battle took only a few moments. After David chose one of his five smooth stones and placed it in the leather yoke of his slingshot, after David let out slack on the cords and twirled his homemade weapon, after that one smooth stone launched like a missile and sank into the giant's forehead, after Goliath stumbled in shock, in disbelief, in the immediate throes of death—only then did the battle end with a thud as this nearly ten-foot-tall giant of a man collapsed at David's feet. The narrative account then sums up this result by seeming to restate what we already know. "So David triumphed over the Philistine with only a sling and a stone, for he had no sword" (1 Samuel 17:50).

Why remind us that David had no sword, that he only used a sling and a stone?

Simply stated, David defeated the giant without what others would describe as the necessary tools. In other words, he overcame Goliath without the resources, tools, instruments, or weapons that everyone expected him to have needed. Saul didn't think David stood a chance against such an enormous, experienced warrior—with or without the proper equipment. I believe it's a safe assumption that every member of the Israelite army, including three of David's brothers, assumed they were watching their kid brother choose a suicide mission.

Anointed by the same Spirit within David that day, you don't need a sword, a spear, a javelin, a shield, or the king's armor. You do not need what people perceive as a requirement for victory. God will enable you to overcome the giants of your generation with what you already have!

So get ready to defeat the enemy of your God in a spiritual battle already ordained by His divine will and perfect purpose. Get ready to experience your greatest breakthrough, get ready to overcome what everyone else says cannot be done, get ready to step into a season of fulfillment and favor—without the sword.

Even without that connection, that network, that relationship, that app, that platform, that recommendation, that training, that degree, or that resource, not only will you overcome, not only will you survive, but you will thrive for the glory of Jesus!

Let me say it again: God will enable you to overcome with what you have!

Stop worrying about what's missing.

Start running toward your giant with what you already have.

What do you have?

You have a faith that moves mountains.

You have a shout that brings down walls.

You have joy that cannot be explained.

You have peace that passes all understanding.

You have a grace that is sufficient, an anointing that destroys the yoke, a gift that cannot be revoked, a destiny that cannot be stopped, a purpose that will be fulfilled, and a love that expels all fear. You walk in mercies that are new every morning. You have the love of the Father, the strength of the Son, and the anointing of the Holy Spirit. You have everything you need and more!

Giants in the Valley

David's confidence in the authority, power, and goodness of the living God did not suddenly spike out of nowhere that day on the battlefront when faced with Goliath. As the youngest of eight brothers, he had likely endured his share of sibling rivalry—if not family trauma—from his brothers. While my conjecture is speculative, we see evidence for how David was regarded by the fact that his family, including his father, overlooked his absence when Samuel came to visit. Only when God prompted Samuel to persist did Jesse send for his youngest son, who was hard at work tending the family's flocks.

On top of this, we have the treatment David received from three of his older brothers, particularly the eldest, Eliab, when he arrived at the battlefront. Obeying his father's instruction to bring provisions to them and then outraged by the blasphemous attitude of Goliath, David was rebuked and labeled as conceited and wicked at heart. He was dismissed by Saul and treated as if he were a child trying to play dress-up.

When refusing Saul's armor, David also revealed that he had already experienced plenty of dangerous situations while shepherding his sheep. He mentions lions and bears—plural—that he had killed before they could harm him or his flock. And despite being young and inexperienced, despite being ridiculed by those around him, David knew what he had—the presence of God's Spirit within him because of his anointing.

We see a different, more poetic expression of this spiritual confidence in one of David's best-known psalms. Drawing on the natural imagery of the hillsides where he tended his sheep, David composed the prayer of praise we know as Psalm 23. He knew if he felt responsible for the feeding, protection, and care of animals as vulnerable as sheep, how much more must God love, protect, and nourish us as our Good Shepherd.

David knew that even when horrendous storms descended and hungry beasts attacked, God was still with him, protecting him and guiding him, providing all he needed each day. David wrote, "Even when I walk through the darkest valley, I will not be afraid, for you are close beside me. Your rod and your staff protect and comfort me" (Psalm 23:4 NLT). Notice that David said, "I will not be afraid" rather than "I never experience fear." As human as you and I are, David surely felt the surge of reactive adrenaline course through his body when facing those dark valleys, those lions and bears. But because of his complete trust in God, David knew he did not have to succumb to his fear. He had the confidence to face them, to fight the source of them.

Following his example, you don't have to pretend you're not afraid. You merely have to choose how you respond to your fears. Will you allow them to consume you? Will you run away when the giant in the valley begins to taunt you? Or will you confront the giant and run toward the opportunity to overcome him?

High Five

If you are going through a dark valley right now, you can put a smile on your face, because it means that God has anointed you to bring down a giant that has been harassing your family and your generation. With your anointing comes authority, power, and purpose to defeat any giant who threatens to darken your valley and steal your joy.

How do I know this? Because of another small but significant detail we must not overlook in the battle between David and Goliath: Why five stones when he needed only one?

It's simple—David prepared for more than just one fight!

For all David knew, Goliath might have brothers in the Philistine army just as large and fierce, brothers waiting to leap into battle if needed. For all David knew, the Philistine army might be so enflamed by losing their greatest warrior that they would rush into battle in retaliation. We know the opposite, in fact, happened:

> When the Philistines saw that their hero was dead, they turned and ran. Then the men of Israel and Judah surged forward with a shout and pursued the Philistines to the entrance of Gath and to the gates of Ekron. Their dead were strewn along the Shaaraim road to Gath and Ekron. When the Israelites returned from chasing the Philistines, they plundered their camp.
>
> David took the Philistine's head and brought it to Jerusalem; he put the Philistine's weapons in his own tent.
>
> 1 Samuel 17:51–54

David selected five stones even though he only needed one.

You also have stones for more than one battle.

You have the stone you need for the giant right in front of you—and the one behind him.

You have a stone for every giant that will dare come your way.

If another giant rises up, you're ready.

If another giant rises up after that, you're still ready.

If another giant rises up, no problem—you're still ready.

You may be tempted to focus only on today's giant, but you have been given more than one stone for your battles. You can rest in the confidence of your anointing because God has you. He wants you to use what you have at your disposal rather than worry about what others expect or want to label you.

So let me ask: Are you a "one stone" Christian?

Are you a "one stone" believer?

Or do you rest in the confidence of having more than what you need for all the battles ahead? Jesus told His followers, "I have given you authority to trample on snakes and scorpions and to overcome all the power of the enemy; nothing will harm you" (Luke 10:19). Whose authority do you have? You have the authority of Jesus Christ, the risen Son of God!

With this authority in your anointing, you have more than one stone—and more even than five stones. You have everything you need to overcome every lion, bear, snake, scorpion, demon, disease, and disaster! Paul reminds us of the victory Christ has won for us, the victory at the core of the authority Jesus has given us:

> The sting of death is sin, and the power of sin is the law. But thanks be to God! He gives us the victory through our Lord Jesus Christ.
>
> Therefore, my dear brothers and sisters, stand firm. Let nothing move you. Always give yourselves fully to the work of the Lord, because you know that your labor in the Lord is not in vain.
>
> 1 Corinthians 15:56–58

In light of what you have been given by Jesus, in light of what God has done for you, in light of the anointing of the Holy Spirit dwelling within you, here's what you must understand:

You are not a one-stone Christian.

You are not a one-stone believer.

You are not a one-stone follower of Jesus.

You have more than just one.

You were not anointed only to slay one giant.

You have enough stones to slay every giant that comes your way.

That giant in your family is coming down.

You have a stone for the giant in your health.

You have a stone for the giant in your finances.

You have a stone for the giant in your past, the giant in your present, and the giant in your future.

You have a stone for every giant that would dare rise up against your children and your children's children.

You have a stone for every battle you will ever face!

So don't worry about running out of stones. Why? Because you know where to find the stream. If you ever run out of stones, no worries. As long as streams of mercy continue to flow, you know where to find more stones.

As long as God is on the throne, as long as Jesus is Lord, as long as you have access to the throne room of grace through the blood of Jesus, as long as the Holy Spirit is still moving, you will never run out of stones!

Corner Stones

Because you are called to defeat every giant in every dark valley, you are called to pick up the stones in the stream right beside you. "When they walk through the Valley of Weeping, it will become a place of refreshing springs. The autumn rains will clothe it with blessings" (Psalm 84:6 NLT). When you live in your anointing, your tears become refreshing springs in a stream of blessing.

And what are the stones available to you in this divinely transformed stream? It's no coincidence that I can think of five!

Stone 1: The Name of Jesus

We have been given authority, power, provision, and protection through the name of Jesus. "I tell you the truth, anyone who believes in me will do the same works I have done, and even greater works, because I am going to be with the Father. You can ask for anything in my name, and I will do it, so that the Son can bring glory to the Father. Yes, ask me for anything in my name, and I will do it!" (John 14:12–14 NLT).

Stone 2: The Word of God

We overcome because God's Word carries power as the ultimate authority of His truth. "For the word of God will never fail" (Luke 1:37 NLT).

Stone 3: The Blood of the Lamb

We overcome because Jesus is the Lamb of God who shed His blood on the cross for our sins. "And they have defeated him by the blood of the Lamb and by their testimony" (Revelation 12:11 NLT).

Stone 4: The Anointing of the Holy Spirit

We received the anointing of the Holy Spirit within us, teaching us truth. "But you have received the Holy Spirit, and he lives within you, so you don't need anyone to teach you what is true. For the Spirit teaches you everything you need to know, and what he teaches is true—it is not a lie. So just as he has taught you, remain in fellowship with Christ" (1 John 2:27 NLT).

Stone 5: The Faith That Overcomes the World

Our faith in God empowers us to overcome the world and to achieve victory through Christ. "For everyone born of God overcomes the world. This is the victory that has overcome the world, even our faith" (1 John 5:4). We will explore these five stones and other resources in the next chapter, but for now, what I'm asking you to do is to shift your spiritual perspective to see that you have more than one stone.

You need to act like you have the five stones, talk like you have the five stones, worship like you have the five stones, breathe like you have the five stones, relax like you have the five stones, and celebrate like you have five stones!

Your victory is assured.

You have more than one stone.

Your anointing equips you for every battle.
You are equipped to slay every giant in your path!

Selecting Your Stone

By now you know how this section works. It's called "Selecting Your Stone" not only because it references David's weapon of choice and victory over Goliath but also, as you now know, because you have limitless spiritual resources you can access through your anointing. Use these questions to reflect on the reality that you are not limited by what you see, by what others say, or by the power of your adversaries. You have more than one stone!

The best way to select the stone you need right now is to enter into the refreshing stream of the Holy Spirit within you. Consider the areas where you feel vulnerable and ask the Spirit to provide whatever you need for the battles ahead—rest, nourishment, reassurance, the peace and protection of your Good Shepherd. Spend a few minutes in prayer and receive all that God's Spirit has for you.

1. When have you felt unprepared, unequipped, or overwhelmed by an unexpected situation, crisis, or confrontation? How did you handle this incident and keep going?

2. When have you experienced a giant and realized God had already equipped you with exactly the stone you needed in order to triumph? What did you learn about your anointing from this experience?

3. What spiritual stones have you collected over the course of your journey of faith? How has God uniquely equipped you to overcome the obstacles you encounter as you live out your divine purpose?

Thank You, God, for walking with me through each dark valley and equipping me with all I need to slay every giant I face. Remind me through the anointing of Your Spirit within me that I need not be a victim of my fear, but I can push through it and rest in the security of Your authority, power, and goodness. Grant me courage to run toward the battles ahead rather than being afraid of uncertainty, because I know I will see Your goodness, Lord, in the land of the living, just as You promised in Psalm 27. Draw me closer so that I may dwell in complete confidence of my anointing through the authority and power of Your Spirit. In Jesus' name, Amen.

6

Close-Range Attacks

Winning Personal Battles and Immediate Struggles

Whether you face attacks from obvious enemies or unexpected assailants, you are not alone. Your anointing by the Lord of heaven's armies assures your victory!

Those who know me know that I'm an incredible *Star Trek* nerd. As a Trekkie, I'm thrilled by the ongoing proliferation of shows, movies, and streaming series derived from creator Gene Roddenberry's imagination. Space is indeed our final frontier, and thanks to quality storytelling in prequels and sequels such as *The Next Generation*, *Deep Space Nine*, *Picard*, and *Strange New Worlds*, the Federation lives on.

Being the lifelong fan that I am, however, none compares to my love for the original series. The seventy-nine episodes of the original *Star Trek* immersed me in a world where science, another of my passions, often intersected with the unpredictable, unexpected, illogical, irrational, and emotional facets of the human condition. Perhaps no other relationship reflects this as well as the one between Captain James T. Kirk, the fiercely courageous and sometimes reckless leader of the Starship *Enterprise*, and his first officer, the half-Vulcan and half-human logistician, Mr. Spock.

Portrayed by actors William Shatner and Leonard Nimoy, respectively, Kirk and Spock often locked horns over major decisions, complementing and balancing each other's natural tendencies. Captain Kirk embodied passion, instinct, and physical action while Mr. Spock relied on science, logic, and intellect. In one of my favorite episodes, "The *Enterprise* Incident," the tension between the two reaches a crisis when Kirk seems to lose control of his faculties, emotions, and self-control.

The episode begins in unique fashion, with First Medical Officer Dr. McCoy narrating the entry in the ship's log instead of the usual introduction by Captain Kirk. The reason for this change becomes evident as McCoy describes how Kirk has grown increasingly edgy, nervous, irrational, and short-tempered with his crew. The doctor diagnoses Kirk as suffering from stress and fatigue due to weeks without time off to relax. Viewers then see for themselves Kirk's behavior in action as he orders the *Enterprise* forward into Romulan airspace, an impulsive, personal directive rather than a Federation order.

Surrounded by enemy vessels and forced to accept defeat, Kirk and Spock are beamed aboard the Romulan commander's ship, where Kirk loses control in an emotional meltdown. Due to Kirk's fit of rage, paranoia, and resistance, Spock relieves his commanding officer of his duty as captain and assumes control, much to the Romulan commander's approval. As Kirk berates Spock for being a traitor, their confrontation culminates with Spock rendering a "Vulcan death-grip" on Kirk, killing him on the spot.

While the unexpected scene is shocking, there's more to the story. Beamed back aboard the *Enterprise*, Kirk not only recovers but reveals his emotional breakdown and faked death are part of a Federation-sanctioned mission to find and acquire a cloaking device, their enemy's latest technology. By the end of the episode, as you might expect, the cloaking device has been located and used to help the *Enterprise* escape with everyone safely aboard, including Spock and a back-to-normal Captain Kirk.

One Up, One Down

Not all difficult relationships work out as smoothly and predictably as Kirk and Spock's. Many, especially when a power dynamic is involved, become weighted with tension compounded again and again. Eventually, the balance of power shifts and jealousy, resentment, rage, and violence characterize the relationship. Such is the case with David and Saul.

While we might assume that their battlefront interaction prior to David's triumph over Goliath was when Saul and David met, based on what we read during the narrative sequence in 1 Samuel, they were actually acquainted before then. During this encounter, Saul dismissed David as young and inexperienced in battle. But apparently, David did indeed have some experience—as Saul's armor bearer! This job was still not the start of their relationship. Their relationship began because of David's skill as a musician.

As Saul began to suffer the consequences of disobeying God, he was plagued by an evil spirit, which led his advisers to suggest music therapy. "Let our lord command his servants here to search for someone who can play the lyre. He will play when the evil spirit from God comes on you, and you will feel better" (1 Samuel 16:16). Saul agreed, and one of his servants recommended none other than Jesse's youngest son from Bethlehem, extolling David to be not only a talented harp player but also "a brave man and a warrior. He speaks well and is a fine-looking man. And the Lord is with him" (1 Samuel 16:18).

> Then Saul sent messengers to Jesse and said, "Send me your son David, who is with the sheep." So Jesse took a donkey loaded with bread, a skin of wine and a young goat and sent them with his son David to Saul.
>
> David came to Saul and entered his service. Saul liked him very much, and David became one of his armor-bearers. Then Saul sent word to Jesse, saying, "Allow David to remain in my service, for I am pleased with him."
>
> Whenever the spirit from God came on Saul, David would take up his lyre and play. Then relief would come to Saul; he would feel better, and the evil spirit would leave him."
>
> 1 Samuel 16:19–23

Several surprising details of their relationship jump out of this passage. Not only did Saul know David, but he loved the young man very much and was so pleased that he asked Jesse's permission for David to remain at court as the king's armor bearer. In addition to being responsible for the royal armor, David would play the harp to soothe Saul when he became troubled, causing the tormenting spirit to go away. These details matter because they emphasize the contrast between these two men already established before their first encounter.

God had expressed His displeasure with Saul to Samuel and sent the prophet to Bethlehem to anoint Saul's successor, the next king. God had revealed David to be His choice, making it clear that even though others overlooked the young shepherd, God saw his heart. While David did not immediately assume the throne, he did immediately receive his anointing and the Holy Spirit. Despite remaining in relative obscurity, David apparently developed a stellar reputation—as a musician, a warrior, a handsome young man with good judgment, one exuding God's presence—at least based on the recommendation provided by Saul's servant. Simply put, David was everything Saul was not.

Their lives intersected going in opposite directions, one up and one down.

David's life was ascending while Saul's life was descending.

David was a young, handsome, humble shepherd from Bethlehem.

Saul was an older, weary, and self-important king from Jerusalem.

David had been chosen to be the next king and anointed by God's Spirit.

Saul had been rejected as king and God's Spirit had departed from him.

David had an outstanding reputation—warrior, musician, poet, anointed.

Saul had a terrible reputation—disobedient, narcissistic, tormented, God-less.

Their opposite trajectories resulted in a curious imbalance in the power of their relationship. For all his authority and power over Israel, Saul was forced to rely on David's musical talent to drive away the tormenting spirit. For all his renown as a handsome warrior, musician, man of God, and future king, David had no public authority or power. No wonder then, even without suffering the tormenting spirit, that Saul's love and dependence on David curdled into jealousy, resentment, and hatred.

Subtle Shade from Jealous Eyes

Ironically, David's victory over Goliath became the last straw in shifting Saul's perspective on the young man who had been serving as his private harpist and royal armor bearer. As king, Saul celebrated David's triumph despite not believing in him before the showdown and despite David's refusal to wear the king's armor. But even in recognizing David's win, Saul's passive-aggressive stance emerges. "As soon as David returned from killing Goliath, Abner brought him to Saul with the Philistine's head still in his hand. 'Tell me about your father, young man,' Saul said. And David replied, 'His name is Jesse, and we live in Bethlehem'" (1 Samuel 17:57–58 NLT).

We already know Saul refused to take David seriously, but here he acts as though he doesn't even recognize David or remember who he is and where he's from. Rather than comment on the obvious trophy in the young giant-slayer's hand, Saul seems to want David's genealogical pedigree. There's some subtle shade here on Saul's part, at least in my twenty-first-century interpretation.

Despite David's triumphant defeat of the once unstoppable Philistine, Saul implies that David was previously a nobody, at least no one from a wealthy family at court or in the royal army. "Oh, yes, now who are you? And where are you from? Who's your father?" Now that David had won this battle he should not have been able to win, Saul sends for David and wants to know about his father—the same father, Jesse, with whom Saul had previously communicated regarding David's appointment as armor bearer and harpist.

Perhaps the king was just rattled and confused, but nonetheless, the gaps in his favor toward the young warrior were starting to show. After David scored such an unexpected win, Saul naturally gave the young man more responsibility and apparently some compensation. But the cracks of comparison soon shattered inside Saul's fragile ego as word of David's extraordinary victory began to spread.

> Whatever Saul asked David to do, David did it successfully. So Saul made him a commander over the men of war, an appointment that was welcomed by the people and Saul's officers alike.

> When the victorious Israelite army was returning home after David had killed the Philistine, women from all the towns of Israel came out to meet King Saul. They sang and danced for joy with tambourines and cymbals. This was their song:
>
> "Saul has killed his thousands,
> and David his ten thousands!"
>
> This made Saul very angry. "What's this?" he said. "They credit David with ten thousands and me with only thousands. Next they'll be making him their king!" So from that time on Saul kept a jealous eye on David.
>
> 1 Samuel 18:5–9 NLT

Saul could not ignore that David's popularity with the people of Israel now outshone his own. The king likely felt humiliated when he heard women throughout the land dancing and singing David's praises by comparing his victories to Saul's. You can almost hear the snarl in Saul's rhetorical question of "What's this?" Because he clearly knew what it was indeed—a threat to his power base and royal authority as king of Israel.

Sometimes your anointing will lead you into close-range attacks you expect. And sometimes your anointing leads into close-range attacks you don't see coming.

Anticipating Your Enemy's Arsenal

David had already faced an imminent close-range attack from Goliath's arsenal. After all, Goliath was a Philistine, a sworn enemy of the Israelites from whom David would expect nothing less than a barrage of weapons. You'll recall that moments before slaying the giant with one perfectly placed stone, David told the Philistine, "You come against me with sword and spear and javelin, but I come against you in the name of the LORD Almighty, the God of the armies of Israel, whom you have defied" (1 Samuel 17:45).

With these three opposing weapons, as with virtually all aspects of David's life, we find symbolic wisdom for our own application. A sword was inherently a close-range weapon, one that required close proximity in order to wound or kill an opponent. The sword represents close-range, immediate attacks, often targeting our personal weaknesses, emotions, or thoughts. These are direct assaults on our identity, self-worth, or faith. Just as a sword requires close contact, these attacks come in the form of self-doubt, shame, or fear, challenging our trust in God in the most personal ways.

Sometimes these close-range assaults are what we expect from those who oppose us. When others make it clear that they despise us, distrust us, and are disgusted by us, we expect to be targeted. Whether they oppose our values, our faith, our character, our experience, our skin color, our social status, or our anointing, we know they're coming for us and are intent on harming us. And how do we prepare?

We prepare by stepping out in faith to meet them and relying on the everlasting promises in the Word of God. We are equipped by our anointing to put on the armor of faith that's always available to us. "Take up the shield of faith, with which you can extinguish all the flaming arrows of the evil one. Take the helmet of salvation and the sword of the Spirit, which is the word of God" (Ephesians 6:16–17).

We wield the sword of truth, sharper than any two-edged blade, to cut through the false accusations, prejudiced assumptions, and unwarranted charges made by those against us. We use God's Word to defend against personal doubts or lies from the enemy. The unassailable fabric of our faith based on the bedrock truth of Scripture provides immediate defense and affirmation of our identity in Christ.

The spear, as a long-distance weapon, represents spiritual attacks from farther away. These longer-range weapons could mean lingering issues from the past, generational challenges, or external influences like societal pressures, relationships, or negative voices around us. This weapon is an attempt to have an impact on us indirectly by casting doubt or creating fear through external circumstances that might be beyond our immediate control.

The enemy might use a spear from social media, a trolling comment from someone you've never met, to try to undermine the confidence of your anointing. A spear might come in the form of an ethnic slur, derogatory comment, or religious remark made by someone in authority over you, such as a supervisor, manager, boss, teacher, or even a pastor. Spears try to get under your skin and upset your equilibrium, causing you to doubt, worry, and lose sight of what's true.

But you don't need to worry about spears when you stand firm on God's promise of victory and protection. "'No weapon forged against you will prevail, and you will refute every tongue that accuses you. This is the heritage of the servants of the LORD, and this is their vindication from me,' declares the LORD" (Isaiah 54:17). You can trust in God's promise that no external weapon, influence, or past issue can ultimately succeed against you. You're empowered to refute and resist these attacks by your inheritance in God's protection through the anointing presence of the Holy Spirit.

The javelin, as a projectile, symbolizes sudden and unexpected attacks that catch us off guard, perhaps in areas we thought were secure. These can be spiritual setbacks, unforeseen trials, or sudden temptations designed to destabilize us. The enemy might use javelin-like attacks to instill anxiety or undermine our confidence when we least expect it.

Javelins are unexpected assaults that rely on surprise and their long-range trajectory to wound us or pin us in place. They might come in the form of an addiction or habitual problem we thought we had overcome only to find our resolve in recovery undermined. Javelins might emerge from unexpected circumstances—a rescinded invitation, canceled trip, or misunderstood motive—that thwart our plans, cause disappointing delays, or deplete our resources.

To defend against the threat of a javelin harming us or pinning us in place, we take refuge in God's faithfulness and protection, knowing He shields us from sudden attacks and covers us with His presence. The confidence that God is our refuge keeps us steady even in unexpected challenges. "He will cover you with his feathers, and under his wings you will find refuge; his faithfulness will be your shield and rampart. You will not fear the terror of night, nor the arrow that flies by day" (Psalm 91:4–5).

Spears and Fears of a Madman

Just as David wasn't surprised by Goliath's multiple weapons, you shouldn't be surprised when obvious enemies reveal their intentions. Unfortunately, those opposing us don't always reveal their true colors until we feel the injury from their unexpected attack. When a personal friend betrays your trust by sharing something you told him or her in confidence, you feel it. When a friendly team member throws you under the bus after a failed project at work, you feel it. When a ministry partner falsely discredits your character to elevate his or her standing, you feel it.

You feel the pain of their assaults because you didn't see them coming. Not from them, not from that direction.

David experienced this kind of subversive attack from the man who initially loved him very much, enjoyed his soothing music, and celebrated his victory over Goliath and the Philistines. Instead, Saul became more and more unhinged and allowed his insecurity and self-absorption to fuel jealousy, resentment, and violence.

> The very next day a tormenting spirit from God overwhelmed Saul, and he began to rave in his house like a madman. David was playing the harp, as he did each day. But Saul had a spear in his hand, and he suddenly hurled it at David, intending to pin him to the wall. But David escaped him twice.
>
> Saul was then afraid of David, for the LORD was with David and had turned away from Saul. Finally, Saul sent him away and appointed him commander over 1,000 men, and David faithfully led his troops into battle.
>
> David continued to succeed in everything he did, for the LORD was with him. When Saul recognized this, he became even more afraid of him. But all Israel and Judah loved David because he was so successful at leading his troops into battle.
>
> 1 Samuel 18:10–16 NLT

Certainly, Saul's dangerous instability was compounded by the tormenting spirit he suffered as a result of disobeying God. Notice that

David's music no longer soothed the king but instead resulted in a murderous rage. Saul hurled his spear at David, who was unarmed and presumably playing his harp, not once but at least twice, which David avoided both times.

The consequence of these unprovoked attacks spotlights the irony of their power struggle once again because we're told "Saul was then afraid of David." If anyone should be afraid, logically it should be the guy playing the harp dodging the spears of a madman! But we've already seen how David handled fear—by trusting God and refusing to be consumed or paralyzed by it. Instead, Saul becomes afraid of David because the king realizes that the Lord is with David because of his anointing—concurrent with the departure of God's Spirit from Saul due to his disobedience.

Saul then ramped up his attempt to murder David, although in a more subtle fashion—by appointing him in charge of a thousand men and sending him to battle with the Philistines. David faithfully followed the king's orders and continued to succeed in every battle he fought. In fact, David continued to succeed not only in every battle he fought but in everything he did. God's favor blessed David with comprehensive success, which only frightened—and likely enraged—the distraught king even more. To make his misery worse, Saul knew that both Israel and Judah, the northern and southern kingdoms of Israel, loved David because he was so successful.

You Never Fight Alone

You and I can learn by David's example here. Even when experiencing a close-range attack from someone who should be blessing, affirming, and mentoring, David had no fear because he knew he was protected by his anointing. God had chosen him and would continue to cover him with protection against any sword, spear, or javelin that Saul might throw at him. You have the same covering from your anointing in the Holy Spirit.

David knew that if God would empower and equip him to withstand Goliath, then God would empower and equip him to withstand King Saul. David knew that no matter who or what he faced, he was never alone in the battle. Remember the contrast in weapons David exclaimed to Goliath? "You come against me with sword and spear and javelin, but I come against you in the name of the LORD Almighty, the God of the armies of Israel, whom you have defied" (1 Samuel 17:45). David told this giant, "You're charging me with all your sharp weapons of war, but I'm facing you in the name of the Lord of heaven's armies!"

David wanted Goliath to know the same thing Saul quickly figured out: David wasn't fighting his battles alone. In essence, this anointed shepherd-becoming-king said, "I'm not here by myself. I know it looks like I'm here by myself. I know it looks like I don't have the same kind of big, shiny weapons you have. But I'm not here by myself. And the weapons I have will never know defeat!"

I'm here to tell you that whatever you're going through—whatever close-range attack or immediate struggle you may be facing—you are not alone!

Heaven has an army standing behind you, before you, alongside you.

Heaven has an army fighting for you.

You may not see it with your mortal eyes, but you can see it with the eyes of your heart.

When Elisha and his servant were surrounded by an enemy army, Elisha prayed for his servant's eyes to be opened.

> "Don't be afraid," the prophet answered. "Those who are with us are more than those who are with them." And Elisha prayed, "Open his eyes, LORD, so that he may see." Then the LORD opened the servant's eyes, and he looked and saw the hills full of horses and chariots of fire all around Elisha.
>
> 2 Kings 6:16–17

When you're going through a dark valley, when you're facing a giant, when you're dodging spears from those who envy and fear you, you are not alone! In those moments, claim the jubilant promise proclaimed by the psalmist:

> If you say, "The LORD is my refuge,"
> and you make the Most High your dwelling,

no harm will overtake you,
 no disaster will come near your tent.
For he will command his angels concerning you
 to guard you in all your ways;
they will lift you up in their hands,
 so that you will not strike your foot against a stone.

Psalm 91:9–12

You have been anointed with God's Spirit, and He will command His angels concerning you to guard you in all your ways! And aren't His angels ministering spiritual beings sent to serve those who inherit salvation? God sends angels to minister and support those who believe and are anointed in His Spirit. The heavenly host is assigned to protect and assist those who belong to God.

You never fight your battles alone. And backed by heaven's armies, your victory is assured!

Selecting Your Stone

Continue your practice of reflecting on the big ideas in this chapter by using the questions for reflection below. Pay close attention to what resonates for you and where you are in your life. Ask the Holy Spirit to reveal the truths from God's Word, the images from David's story, and their application for the battles you're facing. Then spend some time in prayer, releasing any fears and receiving the assurance of God's promises and your anointing in God's Spirit.

1. When have you experienced an unexpected betrayal, assault, or conflict with someone you thought you could trust? How did your faith provide you with what you needed to dodge errant spears and slay the giant?

2. Of the three weapons described to spiritually attack you—sword, spear, javelin—which one has often wounded you in the past? How are you better equipped and empowered now to deflect or engage with this kind of attack?

3. When have you been aware of God's angels protecting you in a dangerous situation? How did your anointing prevent you from experiencing harm in this battle?

Dear God, so often I feel alone and afraid of the day-to-day challenges I face. Thank You for reminding me that I am never alone, that You are always with me, that Your heavenly armies and angels are with me, guiding and guarding in the midst of every giant. Help me to stand firm in Your promises and deflect any and every weapon the enemy attempts to use against me. Guard me when I'm most vulnerable, when those whom I trust betray me, turn against me, exploit me, and harm me. Like David, I know that Your favor rests in my anointing and that You continue to bless me with new mercies every day. In Jesus' name, Amen.

THIRD STONE

INTEGRITY

Anointed to Slay Your Giants with Power

I pray that the eyes of your heart may be enlightened in order that you may know the hope to which he has called you, the riches of his glorious inheritance in his holy people, and his incomparably great power for us who believe. That power is the same as the mighty strength he exerted when he raised Christ from the dead and seated him at his right hand in the heavenly realms, far above all rule and authority, power and dominion, and every name that is invoked, not only in the present age but also in the one to come.

Ephesians 1:18–21

7

Anointed for More

Progressing from Identity to Integrity to Calling

> The same God who first anoints you with the Holy Spirit will anoint you for your new season in His perfect timing. Let your praise fuel your patience as you move into your next anointing!

Bridges have always fascinated me.

Growing up in Pennsylvania, I certainly enjoyed traversing my fair share of bridges. Philadelphia was only an hour away from where we lived, and it still boasts the most bridges in the state, totaling 591, despite Pittsburgh's famous reputation as the "City of Bridges" coming in at 446.[1] One of my childhood favorites was the Ben Franklin Bridge, a multilane suspension bridge across the Delaware River connecting Philly to Camden, New Jersey. I loved starting in one state and then crossing a bridge just under two miles long and ending up in a different one.

1. Mark Houser, "Does Pittsburgh Really Have More Bridges Than Any Other City?," *Pittsburgh*, March 16, 2022, https://www.pittsburghmagazine.com/does-pittsburgh-really-have-more-bridges-than-any-other-city/.

Anytime our family drove across the Ben Franklin or, really, any bridge, I experienced a hybrid emotion comprised of sheer excitement and utter terror, akin to riding a roller coaster or other adrenaline-inducing ride at an amusement park. Looking back, I suspect my excitement resulted from the sense of being suspended at such a height overlooking water, which also induced fear that it might somehow collapse and plunge us into those liquid depths below. As I grew older, my analytical brain assuaged my fears by focusing on the bridge's supports and the engineering intricacy of how it was put together. Looking down at the river below, I'd feel my stomach sink and distract myself by wondering, How much weight could those suspension cables support? Where were the stress points for each beam, pier, or support pillar? What were the bridge's strongest and weakest points from one side to the other?

At this stage of my life, I still love studying how bridges are designed, but I may love the symbolic value of bridges even more. In my ministry and everything I do, I've always considered myself a bridge builder who connects people together rather than a defense contractor who is busy putting up walls to separate them. Bridges also symbolize transition, a link from one point to another, from one season to the next, from our current stage to the next level. If change is inevitable, then we are constantly crossing bridges.

Bridges symbolize connection, inclusion, and cooperation as well as passage, motion, and momentum. That explains why I also associate bridges with the anointings of the Holy Spirit in our lives. Yes, you read that correctly—*anointings*, plural. Because not only are we anointed with the Holy Spirit when we first accept God's gift of salvation through the sacrifice of His Son, Jesus, on the cross, but we also experience the Spirit's anointing at other key intervals of our lives. We see this in the life of David, and perhaps even more importantly, we also see this in the life of Jesus during His time on earth.

David was anointed three times.

Jesus was anointed three times.

Their anointings provide a blueprint for the bridges you will cross to your next anointing.

Anointed to Affirm Your Identity

Throughout Scripture, in both the Old and New Testaments, God anoints those He chooses. As we've seen, David was first anointed by the prophet Samuel while he was still a young shepherd, marking David as God's chosen king. Rather than selecting someone whom people would choose or expect to lead the nation of Israel, God looked into the hearts of prospective leaders and chose David. His anointing signified God's selection and promise for David's future, affirming David's divine identity. "So as David stood there among his brothers, Samuel took the flask of olive oil he had brought and anointed David with the oil. And the Spirit of the LORD came powerfully upon David from that day on" (1 Samuel 16:13 NLT).

It's significant that David received his first anointing in an intimate setting, his father's house in his hometown of Bethlehem, rather than a dramatic public event. Jesus also experienced His first anointing in a deeply personal event, His baptism by John the Baptist, where the Holy Spirit descended on Him like a dove, publicly affirming His identity as the Son of God—which apparently only involved a few witnesses.

> As soon as Jesus was baptized, he went up out of the water. At that moment heaven was opened, and he saw the Spirit of God descending like a dove and alighting on him. And a voice from heaven said, "This is my Son, whom I love; with him I am well pleased."
>
> Matthew 3:16–17

What a beautiful and powerful moment! Not only does the Holy Spirit descend like a dove upon Jesus, but His Father in heaven gives Jesus affirmation of His identity—God's Son—and their relationship—beloved and blessed.

It's no coincidence that immediately after His divine anointing and affirmation, the Spirit directed Jesus into the wilderness for forty days in order to pray and fast—and to be tested by the enemy (see Matthew 4:1–11). Jesus received His anointing in the Spirit but did not immediately begin His public ministry. Instead, He endured a time of intense growth and purposeful preparation. Knowing that Jesus had been fasting, the devil tempted Jesus with food, with authority, and with power—all while attempting to undermine Jesus' identity as God's Son and His mission to minister and pay the price for our sins on the cross. Jesus rebuked the enemy and relied on the truth of God's Word for His rebuttals, revealing His shrewd wisdom and supernatural insight within the fullness of His humanity.

Similarly, David did not immediately ascend the throne following his first anointing. Even though Samuel anointed David, making it evident both externally—using the olive oil the prophet had brought with him—and internally—as the Spirit of the Lord came upon David with power in that moment—David did not immediately begin his reign as king. David was anointed but still had to wait until God's chosen time before replacing Saul as king. Having to wait also meant that David had to serve Saul until God revealed His appointed time, which wasn't easy, as we saw in our last chapter. Like Jesus in the wilderness, David endured a time of testing and experiential preparation as a bridge leading to his next anointing.

While he served Saul and waited on God's timing, David did not become entitled, wait around passively, or assume nothing was required of him now that he had been anointed. Instead, David served as a harpist, soldier, and military leader for King Saul, a man who quickly came to despise David's youth, anointing, and reputation. We're told, "Whatever Saul asked David to do, David did it successfully" (1 Samuel 18:5 NLT).

While Saul, in fits of rage, threw spears at David and sent him to the battlefronts in hopes that David would be killed, David had to survive physically, emotionally, socially, and politically. To further complicate the strained relationship between David and Saul during this period of transition, David experienced a deep, abiding friendship with Saul's son Jonathan (see 1 Samuel 18:1–4) and eventually married Saul's daughter Michal, who loved her new husband very much (see 1 Samuel 18:27).

Both David and Jesus were chosen by God, and their anointings were a personal affirmation of God's special purpose for them. Just as David and Jesus were chosen, we, too, are chosen by God to fulfill His purposes in our lives. God anointed each of them in a uniquely personal way followed by a time of testing and preparation before their second anointing, which He continues to do with each of us today.

God anoints you personally before He anoints you publicly. He anoints you in a safe, intimate setting before He anoints you in the presence of your enemies. He anoints you and often requires you to wait before He anoints you to take urgent action.

While you may grow impatient, your second anointing is always worth the wait.

Anointed to Praise

If God's first anointing affirms your identity, then the second anointing confirms your calling. David's second anointing took place when he was made king over the tribe of Judah. This anointing was a step toward his eventual kingship over all Israel and signified his role as a leader and servant of God's people. "Then the men of Judah came to Hebron, and there they anointed David king over the tribe of Judah" (2 Samuel 2:4).

After waiting years for his turn to lead, David finally got his shot when King Saul died. David went from a personal anointing to a public anointing. Please keep in mind, however, that while he was anointed to be king of Judah, David was not yet anointed to be king over all of Israel. Basically, his second anointing allowed him to occupy a portion of what God had promised him before he was anointed to lead over all of that divine promise. Consider, too, that Judah literally means "praise," and in David's case, this emphasizes how our praise becomes the bridge to our power.

God may anoint you and make you a steward of a portion of your promise to see if you are faithful in the small things before He entrusts you with responsibility for the big things. If He sees you can manage all that's entrusted to you, if He watches you lead with integrity and grow into maturity, then He knows you're on your way to fulfilling all of your divine purpose. In the meantime, however, you are anointed to praise Him in all that you do—your thoughts, words, and actions.

You are called to serve and glorify God. You shouldn't expect to rule over all of your Israel until you learn to rule over your Judah. You are anointed for praise before you fulfill your promise with purposeful power!

With Jesus' second anointing, we find someone offering Him praise and giving thanks for His love, mercy, and forgiveness. His second anointing reveals something of the scandal of the Gospel message when a sinful woman anointed His feet with expensive perfume, symbolizing His mission to serve and save the sinners, the outcasts, those despised and rejected by others.

> A woman in that town who lived a sinful life learned that Jesus was eating at the Pharisee's house, so she came there with an alabaster jar of perfume. As she stood behind him at his feet weeping, she began to wet his feet with her tears. Then she wiped them with her hair, kissed them and poured perfume on them.
>
> Luke 7:37–38

Her reputation was known by those dining with Jesus, but He rebuked them by contrasting her sincere offering of gratitude, kindness, and hospitality with their self-righteousness, hypocrisy, and judgment. Her act of sacrificial praise foreshadowed our individual response to the way Jesus would die on the cross for all our sins. There is no way we can repay the debt He paid for us except to love Him and surrender our lives to Him, to praise Him. Our response includes humility, a sense of accepting that we are fully forgiven but not yet perfected as we will be with God in heaven after we pass from this life.

David and Jesus were both called to lead and serve God's people. Their second anointings reveal their integrity for leadership and remind us that true leadership in God's Kingdom is characterized by service and humility. In light of how God has saved us, we become servant leaders on a divine mission to share the Good News of Jesus Christ and to advance God's Kingdom on earth as it is in heaven. We become willing to lay down our lives just as Christ gave His life for us. We steward those resources and people entrusted to our care.

Anointed to Fulfill Your Calling

After you've been anointed in the Holy Spirit to establish your new identity in Christ, you are then anointed to grow into the integrity of your calling, your faithfulness as a steward of the resources and position of leadership entrusted to you. As you grow in maturity, you come into the fullness of your calling, fulfilling your divine purpose over all that God has for you.

Once again, we see this in the third anointing of David as well as the third anointing of Jesus. David's third anointing occurred once he became king over all Israel, not just Judah, finally uniting the tribes and establishing his reign over the nation in its entirety. "When all the elders of Israel had come to King David at Hebron, the king made a covenant with them at Hebron before the LORD, and they anointed David king over Israel" (2 Samuel 5:3).

We find Jesus anointed for a third time just prior to His crucifixion when Mary anointed Him with perfume in preparation for His burial, symbolizing His ultimate sacrifice and authority as the King of kings. "Then Mary took about a pint of pure nard, an expensive perfume; she poured it on Jesus' feet and wiped his feet with her hair. And the house was filled with the fragrance of the perfume" (John 12:3). She along with other women later came to the tomb of Jesus on the third day to anoint His corpse with oils and spices only to discover the stone rolled away and their Savior resurrected from the dead. There was no anointing of His body after death—because He rose again!

David's final anointing established his full authority as king, while Jesus' anointing pointed to His sacrificial death and eternal kingship. These anointings remind us of the ultimate authority and kingship of Jesus, who reigns over all.

Both the anointings of David and Jesus highlight their divine selection, mission of service, and ultimate authority. Based on their examples and our commitment to Christ, we are called to recognize and embrace our anointing in the Holy Spirit, serve God our Father with humility, and acknowledge Jesus as our eternal King. When you walk in the anointing God has placed on your life, you fulfill His purpose in your life, the calling you live out in the full power of the Holy Spirit in all areas of your life.

When you receive the Holy Spirit, you are anointed to affirm your identity, then anointed to gain experience and solidify your integrity, and then anointed to produce good fruit, the fruit of the Spirit. Remember, your anointings have been upgraded exponentially through the finished work of Jesus Christ on the cross. When you abide in the power of the Holy Spirit, your threefold anointing explodes with the dynamic power of God in ways that not only transform you from the inside out but also transform the world around you. Your anointings result in a comprehensive reliance on the grace, gift, and glory of God inside of you that exude the power of the Spirit, the love of the Son, and the goodness of the Father.

In the fulfilled advancement and maturity of your anointings, your life reflects the example of Jesus' ministry on earth as you share His love, do good to others, and heal those oppressed by the enemy. We're reminded that "God anointed Jesus of Nazareth with the Holy Spirit and with power. He went about doing good and healing all who were oppressed by the devil, for God was with him" (Acts 10:38 ESV).

In the advancement of your anointings, you overcome evil and heal the sick. "And they cast out many demons and anointed with oil many who were sick and healed them" (Mark 6:13 ESV).

In the advancement of your anointings, you pray and anoint others. "Is anyone among you sick? Let him call for the elders of the church, and let them pray over him, anointing him with oil in the name of the Lord" (James 5:14 ESV).

In the advancement of your anointings, you do what other people will not do.

In the advancement of your anointings, you do what other people cannot do.

In the advancement of your anointings, there is always more!

But Wait—There's More

You've likely seen infomercials on television or online that sell their products by boasting about feature after feature. And just when you think they've finished the benefits of their incredible product, they exclaim, "But wait—there's more!" This is how I feel about the incredible riches we have when we live in the fullness of our anointings in the Holy Spirit.

Layer after layer of benefits emerge when you live the Spirit-anointed life.

Foremost, you experience a power surge unlike any other. Jesus told His followers, "But you will receive power when the Holy Spirit comes on you; and you will be my witnesses in Jerusalem, and in all Judea and Samaria, and to the ends of the earth" (Acts 1:8). Notice that He did not say you will receive "some power" or "a little bit of power now and then" or "power when you really need it." No! Jesus declared emphatically that when you receive the gift of the Holy Spirit, you receive complete access to the limitless power of the living God!

Power over devils.

Power over sickness.

Power over demons.

Power over addiction.

Power over depression and anxiety.

Power over negative thoughts.

Jesus told us we have been given all the power we need to do what we are created and called to do. "I have given you authority to trample on snakes and scorpions and to overcome all the power of the enemy; nothing will harm you" (Luke 10:19). In the anointings of the Holy Spirit, you are directly part of the ultimate, greatest power source in existence.

If you have the Holy Spirit, you are powerful.

If your family is full of the Holy Spirit, your family is powerful.

If your children are full of the Holy Spirit, your children are powerful.

Because you have the power of the Spirit, stop acting as though you are weak.

Because you have the power of the Spirit, stop talking as though you are weak.

Because you have the power of the Spirit, stop thinking you are weak.

Stop praying as though you are weak.

Stop leading as though you are weak.

Stop loving as though you are weak.

With the Holy Spirit inside you, you are powerful!

With the power of the Holy Spirit also comes freedom. "Now the Lord is the Spirit, and where the Spirit of the Lord is, there is freedom" (2 Corinthians 3:17). Jesus told His followers, "So if the Son sets you free, you will be free indeed. . . . Then you will know the truth, and the truth will set you free" (John 8:36, 32).

In the power of your anointings, you are free!

Free *from* and free *to*.

Free from a life of sin.

Free from condemnation.

Free from shame.

Free from the past.

Free from curses.

Free to occupy His promises.

Free to preach His Word.

Free to do His will.

Free to teach your children.

Free to build.

Free to create.

Free to live!

In the power and freedom of your anointings in the Spirit, you are holy and live in the light. "So I say, walk by the Spirit, and you will not gratify the desires of the flesh" (Galatians 5:16).

You are holy because you are free from darkness and free to walk in the light! "For you were once darkness, but now you are light in the Lord. Live as children of light" (Ephesians 5:8).

You are holy to be whole. "May God himself, the God of peace, sanctify you through and through. May your whole spirit, soul and body be kept blameless at the coming of our Lord Jesus Christ" (1 Thessalonians 5:23).

In the fullness of your anointings, you have victory. "But thanks be to God! He gives us the victory through our Lord Jesus Christ" (1 Corinthians 15:57).

With your anointings comes victory because the same Spirit in you raised Jesus from the dead. "And if the Spirit of him who raised Jesus from the dead is living in you, he who raised Christ from the dead will also give life to your mortal bodies because of his Spirit who lives in you" (Romans 8:11).

You have victory over depression.

You have victory over anxiety.

You have victory over fear.

You have victory over curses.

When you live in the fullness of your anointings, you have all you need forevermore. "As for you, the anointing you received from him remains in you, and you do not need anyone to teach you. But as his anointing teaches you about all things and as that anointing is real, not counterfeit—just as it has taught you, remain in him" (1 John 2:27).

If Jesus is your Savior, if Jesus is your Lord, then the Holy Spirit lives inside you.

Which means your faith, family, and future are full of, fueled by, and furnished with power, freedom, holiness, victory, and anointing! Not later, not sometime ahead. Right now you are entering into a fresh anointing of the Spirit. Regardless of how gigantic Goliath appears, your anointing is always greater.

This season will not be a season of defeat.

This year will not be a year of destruction.

This time will not be a time of despair.

This chapter will not be a chapter of disappointment or disillusionment.

Right now, you and your house will experience the abundance of Christ—His power, freedom, holiness, victory, and anointing.

God anointed His purpose.

God anointed His passion.

God anointed His promise.

God anointed the worshiper.

God anointed the warrior.

God anointed the world changer.

God anointed His identity.

God anointed His integrity.

God anointed His influence.

God has anointed you!

Selecting Your Stone

When you experience the anointing of the Holy Spirit, then you are anointed for more—more power, more blessings, more abundance, more life. As you follow the examples of David and Jesus, you experience more immersion in the advancement of your anointings. You become more reliant on the Spirit within you as your only power source.

Reflect on the impact of your anointings by using the questions below to help you enrich your understanding of the Spirit's role in your life and to advance your relationship with God. Then, spend a few moments opening yourself to the voice of the Spirit as you quiet your mind, take some deep breaths, and still your heart before Him.

1. As you consider the three anointings of David and Jesus, which of the three resonates with where you see yourself in your faith? Do you see God continuing to affirm your identity in Christ, moving you into a portion of your promise, or entrusting to you full responsibility for your calling?

2. What are some ways God has continued to prepare, equip, and train you after your first anointing when you accepted Jesus into your life? How have—or will—these experiences enabled you to embrace your second anointing?

3. When you consider the riches of your anointings, which ones resonate most with where you are in this season of life? What do you most need right now—more power, more freedom, more holiness, more victory, or more anointing?

Dear heavenly Father, thank You for the anointings You have placed on my life. Help me to fully embrace my identity as a new creature in Christ, Your beloved child. Open the eyes of my heart that I may clearly recognize my calling and be the best steward of all entrusted to me. Allow me to advance and serve others with humility as I seek to honor Jesus as my King, my Lord, and my Savior in everything I do. Empower me through Your Spirit to fulfill the unique purpose You have created me to accomplish. With a joyful and thankful heart, I praise and magnify Your holy name! In Jesus' name, Amen.

8

Watch Me

Overcoming by the Blood of the Lamb

> Just as David's anointing empowered him to slay a giant, you will overcome by the power of Christ in you through the Holy Spirit. When others overlook and underestimate your faith, tell them, "Watch me!"

One of the gifts of growing older that I've been blessed to receive is becoming a grandparent. It's a curious experience because I don't feel old enough to be anyone's grandfather, grandpa, *abuelo*, *abuelito*, or *tata*. I quickly learned, however, not to associate my joy at being blessed with the extending of my tribe with the connotations of aging, which so many people view negatively and pessimistically. Instead, I cherish these children of my children and delight in who they are and who they will become.

And I have to say that the perks of being a grandparent are definitely worthwhile. After raising three children of our own, my wife, Eva, and I love being able to host sleepovers and enjoy special events with our grandkids—and then letting them return to their parents until our next visit. We can just focus on loving them and spoiling them without sweating the details as we did when we were parents.

One of the many blessings of being a grandparent I've noticed is perspective. We've lived enough life at this point that Eva and I savor seeing the world through the innocent, fresh eyes of our sweet grandsons and granddaughters. Their curiosity and sense of discovery allows us to experience so many simple joys anew, from collecting shells on the beach to counting stars in the sky, from sharing ice cream cones to cooking meals together. Their openness, honesty, and joyful sense of being in the present moment is contagious.

One of the gifts that my wife and I are privileged to give to our grandchildren is our undivided attention and attuned engagement. We try to make each one of them feel special, seen for their unique and beautiful individuality, as well as affirmed as belonging to our family, our community, and our church family. Giving each child our full attention usually includes being an engaged, supportive witness to their accomplishments in each developmental stage.

When they're babies and toddlers, it's natural to watch closely for each new accomplishment—smiling, rolling over, sitting up, crawling, walking, and talking. We applaud their growth and provide positive reinforcement to encourage their maturation. As they grow older, they learn to expect our praise and affirmation. They develop an awareness of enjoying the attention they receive from us and others and become little performers.

I've noticed that around kindergarten, they like to show off their latest skills, whether it's singing a song, choreographing new dance moves, throwing a baseball, kicking a soccer ball, solving a puzzle, or drawing a picture. They want to be noticed and seen doing something exceptional, something they feel good at doing, something they hope to be validated and affirmed in doing.

I was reminded of this recently when visiting with our youngest granddaughter, who's five years old. She immediately took my hand and my wife's hand and led us to the living room so she could show us her gymnastics routine, including a somersault and handstand. "Watch me!" she said repeatedly, even though our eyes never left her. There was a sense of pride and eagerness to share her accomplishment with us, a subtle longing for us to affirm and bless her skill and style, which we were only too happy to do.

Seeing her exuberance and hearing the urgency in her voice each time she said, "Watch me!" reminded me of David just before his showdown with Goliath. It reminded me of how we as believers need to declare the confidence of our anointing in the Holy Spirit in everything we say and do. Even before we're adults, other people are often quick to criticize, discourage, overlook, and underestimate who we are and what we have been called to do.

All the more reason we must heed the words of Jesus, "Unless you change and become like little children, you will never enter the kingdom of heaven" (Matthew 18:3). All the more reason we must overcome by the power of our anointing and tell others, "Watch me!"

Divine Defiance

The way young children proclaim, "Watch me!" usually does not convey the confident defiance that we find in David's response to those doubting him. When adults demand, "Watch me!" there is usually a brash determination being expressed. These people are often told they may not break the rules, be the exception, or do what is not permissible—to which they retaliate with stubborn persistence.

Divine defiance, as I like to call it, is distinct from the typical refusal to comply. Divine defiance does not break the rules out of spite but rather shatters the feeble expectations of those who would hold them back. Divine defiance expresses humility fused with supernatural power rather than resistance fused with human willpower.

David learned about divine defiance shortly after his first anointing. He had already been almost overlooked by his family, but God saw him and looked into his heart.

The other soldiers said to him, "Have you seen the giant?" (1 Samuel 17:25 NLT). David's oldest brother, Eliab, said to him, "What are you doing around here anyway? . . . I know about your pride and deceit. You just want to see the battle!" (1 Samuel 17:28 NLT). And King Saul told David, "Don't be ridiculous! . . . There's no way you can fight this Philistine and possibly win! You're only a boy, and he's been a man of war since his youth" (1 Samuel 17:33 NLT).

These derogatory discouragements all came before David went face-to-face with Goliath. We would expect, as I suspect David expected, an arrogant enemy to defy us, doubt us, dismiss us—but these were the messages issued from people who were supposedly on David's side. Rather than provide support, encouragement, and affirmation, however, they only compounded the conflict and added unnecessary barriers to the battle.

David was discounted, dismissed, and discouraged from living out his anointing when confronted with the Philistine giant whom everyone else feared and refused to take on. No one—including his own brothers and the king for whom David had already begun serving as harpist and armor bearer—believed in him. But did David allow them to dissuade him from doing what the Spirit of God empowered him to do? No!

Others who should have supported David and helped him to prepare to be king failed him as well. Most notably, David's wife Michal, who just happened to be Saul's daughter, came to resent her husband for numerous reasons, including his infidelity with Bathsheba and his responsibility for the death of Bathsheba's husband, Uriah the Hittite. So when David achieved one of the crowning achievements of his divine mission, returning the Ark of the Covenant to Jerusalem, Michal refused to offer any support. "As the ark of the Lord was entering the City of David, Michal daughter of Saul watched from a window. And when she saw King David leaping and dancing before the Lord, she despised him in her heart" (2 Samuel 6:16).

I suspect there were also plenty of detractors and distractors who did not believe David would ever become king—even after he was anointed to be king of Judah. They likely thought that was as far as David would go. Some were probably still loyal to Saul, who spent the rest of his reign trying to undermine and kill David. When Saul died, David was anointed to reign over Judah, but his enemies refused to believe he would unite all the tribes of Israel and restore the nation, which of course came to pass as well.

You have likely encountered similar discouragement from others too. There are those who are overt about their disdain and contempt of you and your capabilities, and you may have accepted that no matter what you do, they will never be convinced of your anointing to fulfill your divine mission. Then there are those who are covert about their true feelings, often jealousy and envy, and act as though they're for you while plotting against you.

These may be family members—including parents, siblings, spouses, and children—as well as those considered friends, neighbors, coworkers, and even other Christians. They may be motivated out of their own insecurities, resentment, and inability to achieve what they're watching you achieve. They may be compelled out of a sincere desire for what they believe to be best. But regardless of what fuels their failure to support you, they will never have the last word.

Who has the last word?

God! He is the Alpha and Omega, the Author and Finisher of your faith.

When you are anointed by the power of His Spirit, you are empowered for more.

When you are empowered for more, you can live in the confidence of your calling.

When you live in the confidence of your calling, you can tell everyone else, "Watch me!"

Prayer, Praise, and Proclamation

Just as you have been anointed by the same Spirit who dwelled in David, you can defy the logic, rationale, criticism, and doubts of those who underestimate you. Keep in mind that David was just a young man, likely a teenager, with no battle experience, and apparently few people, if any, in his life believed in him. Nonetheless, he would not back down from a confrontation that everyone else refused to even consider. David would not be intimidated by the obnoxious swagger of Goliath. David would not be downcast because of his brother's rebuke. David would not be dismayed by the pride and fear of Saul. Instead, David trusted God and the power of God's Spirit within him—and did what seemed impossible!

David's anointing infused him with boldness—not human arrogance and overconfidence in his own abilities, which was Goliath's method.

Instead of channeling any anger, frustration, or disappointment toward the soldiers, his brothers, or Saul, David focused on the showdown with the giant Philistine disrespecting the God of Israel. David conveyed a message just as loud and fierce as Goliath's boasts, only David's was backed by the power of his anointing. "Sure, you can say I'm too young and inexperienced, too unskilled and unprepared, too naive and idealistic, but you know what? Just watch me! Watch me and witness what God will do through me. You might say I cannot, but I say that God says I can!"

"Watch me!" is your prayer, praise, and proclamation of the power of your anointing.

When you trust in God and rely on His power through your anointing, then your humility and reliance on Him become holy confidence. You turn your human pride inside out and the expectations of others upside down when you live in the power of your anointing. You might be tempted to think that proclaiming, "Watch me!" is too close to pride and personal hubris. But as long as your power source is the Spirit, your example is the Son, and your goal is the Father's glory, "Watch me!" is perhaps the best, most concise declaration of worship, wonder, and wisdom you can utter.

Why do I say this? Just consider . . .

"Watch me!" announces the prophetic expression of radical anointing over someone who has been told, "You can't do it, you won't do it, you don't have what it takes. This task is impossible for anyone to accomplish, but even more so for you."

"Watch me!" conveys the cry of your soul bursting with praise as you experience the peace, power, purpose, and passion of your anointing.

"Watch me!" declares that within you dwells the Holy Spirit, the same Spirit who raised Jesus from the dead. The same Spirit who anointed David so that he could defeat Goliath.

"Watch me!" heralds the present season of your anointing as someone living a grace-filled, Christ-centered, Spirit-led life.

"Watch me!" does not originate in your ego but in God's grace. The message of "Watch me!" reveals someone who knows they are a sinner saved by grace and grace alone. It's the message board announcing that you know you cannot do it on your own but that you can do all things through Christ who strengthens you. It's the bright neon sign lighting the way to your glorious future and your next anointing. It's the vivid fluorescent colored frame showcasing you as God's masterpiece, His trophy of grace, His beloved child in whom He is well pleased.

"Watch me!" signals the security of your power in God's Spirit.

"Watch me!" is the battle cry that topples every giant!

Origin of Your Overcoming

Your anointing in the Holy Spirit, by the Holy Spirit, and through the Holy Spirit is your supernatural source of power. But the origin of your ability to overcome, while certainly reliant on the Spirit, originates with the blood of the Lamb. The basis for this truth comes from God's Word. In the Revelation to John, the disciple glimpses the past, present, and future impact of Christ—the Word made flesh, the Son of God, the Emmanuel, God with us—on humankind. As part of his vision, John heard a loud voice from heaven proclaiming,

> Now have come the salvation and the power
> and the kingdom of our God,
> and the authority of his Messiah.
> For the accuser of our brothers and sisters,
> who accuses them before our God day and night,
> has been hurled down.
> They triumphed over him
> by the blood of the Lamb
> and by the word of their testimony.
>
> Revelation 12:10–11

You are anointed to prove hell wrong by triumphing over the enemy. How? By the blood of the Lamb and the word of your testimony. Your spiritual anointing washes you clean from the spiritual stain of sin so that you are now white as snow. No longer can the devil taunt you as Goliath taunted David. No longer can the devil ensnare you as he attempted to tempt Jesus coming out of the wilderness. No longer can the devil accuse you before God day and night—or any other time!

So often the enemy uses the doubts, discouragement, and criticism of others to undermine not only our confidence but our identity. You may have heard the distinction made between guilt and shame. When you feel guilty, you regret and show remorse for your words and actions, for disobeying God—either by doing something you know is wrong or by leaving undone something right you know you needed to do. Shame sets in, on the other hand, when you feel unworthy, unlovable, and irredeemable because of who you are—not what you've done or left undone. The enemy loves to look for ways to shift guilt, which can often be a healthy response to sinful disobedience within your conscience, to soul-numbing shame, which grows like a toxic mushroom in the darkness of insecurity and isolation.

The way to kill shame is to live in the light of truth. The devil may tempt, taunt, and accuse you of being unlovable, unforgivable, unreachable—but those are lies. Every human being is created in the divine image of God, and every follower of Jesus anointed by the power of His Spirit within them is loved, forgiven, and connected to the supernatural power of the living God. You are saved by grace through the sacrifice of Christ on the cross to pay the debt of your sins. You are a new creation, born again, forgiven, and infused with the gift of the Spirit. You are an overcomer who can refute the accusations of the enemy because you are saved by the blood of the Lamb and the word of your testimony.

You are no longer under the power of sin and death. We're told, "For since death came through a man, the resurrection of the dead comes also through a man. For as in Adam all die, so in Christ all will be made alive" (1 Corinthians 15:21–22). Once you have been saved, you are no longer defined by your past mistakes, failures, and selfish choices. You are now crucified with Christ (see Galatians 2:20), dead to the power of sin in your life (see 2 Corinthians 5:17), and alive in the anointed power of God's Spirit within you (see Romans 8:9).

Your identity is now God's anointed, His chosen, His beloved.

The devil can accuse all he wants, but he can never change the eternal reality of who you are in Christ. You have overcome by the blood of the Lamb and the word of your testimony. It's time to stand out to anyone—including and especially the enemy—who tries to demean, diminish, or destroy you.

Your anointing overcomes every accusation against you!

Anthem of Your Anointing

You are anointed to prove hell wrong by issuing a bold anthem: *Watch me!*

This declaration is both a proactive announcement of your intention to thrive in all areas of your life because of the anointing of the Holy Spirit and a defensive rebuttal to all the doubters, critics, naysayers, trolls, cancelers, skeptics, and dismissers. They say, "Ridiculous! There's no way you will slay that giant, survive that battle, and unite those you lead. You will never make it past the first hurdle."

Just as David heard prior to his greatest victories, these negative declarations of discouragement attempt to inundate, saturate, and captivate your current reality. Without a doubt, every day experience the clamor of confusion, the noise of negativity, the cacophony of criticism, and the din of delusions all communicating that you don't have what's required to overcome the gigantic obstacles before you. These critics turn up their volume in hopes you will despair and give up your faith, abandon God and the hope you have in Christ, and ignore and underestimate the power of the Holy Spirit in your life. Their refrain becomes so predictable:

"You will never defeat the giants in your generation."

"You will never occupy God's promises."

"You will never conquer new territories for Him."

"No way!"

"Never!"

But here's what they don't know, don't believe, or don't want to remember: When you have faith in the finished work of Christ, when you step into every chapter and season of life with the certainty of 2 Corinthians 5:7 that we walk by faith and not by sight, when you live with the sacred algorithm of Romans 10:17 that faith comes from hearing the Good News about Christ, when you stand empowered with the promise of Matthew 21:22 that you can pray for anything, and if you have faith, you will receive it, when you walk and talk, live and give and forgive with *that* faith, with your hope in Christ, and with the faith of Christ, with that mountain-moving, devil-rebuking, demon-binding, atmosphere-shifting, captive-freeing, family-saving, supernatural-powered, overflow-inducing, truth-exalting, light-exposing, chain-breaking, door-opening, my-cup-runneth-over type of faith . . .

Then you can stand up as David did through his actions.

Then you can rise up as David did through his accomplishments.

Then you can speak up as David did through his songs and his psalms.

Then you can slay every giant you encounter, proclaiming just as David did, "Today the LORD will conquer you, and I will kill you and cut off your head. And then I will give the dead bodies of your men to the birds and wild animals, and the whole world will know that there is a God in Israel!" (1 Samuel 17:46 NLT).

And because you are crucified with Christ and now it is Christ living in you (see Galatians 2:20), and because you abide in His Word and His Word abides in you (see John 15:7), and because you are a new creation with Christ as your everything (see 2 Corinthians 5:17; Colossians 3:11), then you have the authority, the faith, and the power to formally respond to all the naysayers, detractors, haters, negative and contrary voices both internal and external that have the audacity to tell you that you will

never overcome your giants,
never occupy your Jerusalem,
never live an abundant life,
never live right with God,
never see your family saved,
never see your body completely healed,
never conquer your dream and possess the promise,
never change the world around you.

Then in the fullness of your anointing in the Holy Spirit, the same Spirit that raised Jesus from the dead back to life, you will tell them that because you are saved by grace through faith, because you are the direct byproduct of everything Jesus paid for on the cross, and because you are completely crucified with Christ and you no longer live but Christ lives in you, "Permit me to utter the following two-word response: Watch me!"

If you have this kind of faith, this kind of power, this kind of hope in your life, then you can open your mouth with authority from heaven and in the fullness of your life in the Spirit and say, "Watch me!"

Watch me overcome by the blood of the Lamb and the word of my testimony (see Revelation 12:11).

Watch me conquer the mountain and possess the promise (see 1 Corinthians 2:9).

Watch me live life abundantly (see John 10:10).

Watch me glorify and magnify Jesus as never before (see 1 Corinthians 10:31).

Watch me and my house serve the Lord (see Joshua 24:15).

Watch me and my family go from glory to glory (see 2 Corinthians 3:18).

Watch me and imitate me as I imitate Christ (see 1 Corinthians 11:1).

Watch me live a holy, healed, healthy, happy, humble, hungry, honoring life (see 1 Peter 1:16).

Watch me as God reveals who He created me to be and who I really am (see Romans 8:19).

Watch me live, forgive, heal, bless, and change the world in the name of Jesus for the glory of Christ (see Romans 1:16).

If you are ready to prove your detractors wrong, and if you are ready to prove hell wrong, then praise like you are ready. Shout like you are ready. Worship like you are ready. Rejoice like you are ready.

You are anointed to prove hell wrong!

"Watch me!" is the anthem of your anointing!

Selecting Your Stone

Once again, use the questions and prayer starter below as an opportunity to still yourself before God, to reconnect with the presence of the

Holy Spirit within you, and to listen to His voice. Eliminate as many of the day's distractions as you can so that you can give God your full, undivided attention. Turn off or at least silence your phone. Close or remove screens from your field of vision. Try to find a place of silence where you won't be interrupted for a few quiet minutes.

Know that you never have to tell God to watch you because your loving heavenly Father never takes His eyes off you. You are His beloved child in whom He is well pleased. You have been given the keys to His Kingdom as you love, serve, and lead in the fullness of your anointing. Allow your holy confidence to be recharged as you receive all the gifts, blessings, and anointings God's Spirit has for you. Remember, He is the reason you can tell others, "Watch me!"

1. When have family members, friends, coworkers, and other believers discouraged you from pursuing your divine mission through the power of your anointing? How will you respond to them differently now than you have in the past?

2. How have your encounters and communications using social media created unnecessary barriers that drain your energy, distract your attention, and deter your spiritual growth? How can you eliminate or at least limit these negative online exchanges?

3. What will others watch you do differently as you now live in the fullness of your anointing? What promises from God's Word do you claim to back up your declaration of divine defiance?

Dear Lord, in the past I have often been discouraged and derailed by the criticisms and false assumptions of others. Forgive me when I have allowed them to slow down my battles and the necessary confrontations with the giants blocking my path. Thank You for all the spiritual riches You pour into my life through the anointing of Your Spirit. May my life be a trophy of Your grace, a triumph over trials as I persevere through the power of Your Spirit and walk in faithful obedience. Never allow me to be discouraged by others but to always remember Your power within me, the basis of my holy confidence to say, "Watch me!" In Jesus' name, Amen.

9

The Word Wins

Running in the Power of God's Word

God not only gives you His Word but also accompanies His Word. When you experience the fullness of your anointing, the power of God's Word lives in you!

While word games often frustrate me, I love a good linguistic challenge.

Some games, like the very popular online game Wordle, rely on players' knowledge of specific words based on a limited number of alphabetic letters provided. You attempt to discover the specific, relevant letters and then arrange them in the correct order to reveal the solution. This can prove more challenging than it sounds.

Other word games require more than just identifying a word from an unknown scramble but necessitate knowing definitions, connotations, and pop culture usage and associations of individual words and word groups.

Perhaps my favorite word games rely on both. Crossword puzzles require the deciphering of word clues to arrive at solutions able to fit the requisite number of letter spaces either down or across. You have to know comprehensive definitions of various words as well as the latest slang, current events, ancient history, and pop culture. This linguistic knowledge must then be filtered through the allocated spaces available for the correct answer. The clue might be, for example, "between children and adults," with five spaces allotted, resulting in the answer "teens."

My frustration mounts when the clues are especially cryptic, misleading, or idiosyncratic. I recall working a recent crossword in which the clue read, "Hostess response to spoiled desserts." The answer contained eight letters and stumped me until I realized the answer was likely embedded in the clue. As I studied each word in the clue, something clicked when I got to the word "desserts" and realized that spelled backward it becomes "stressed." Considered sneaky by some, these clues have helped me enjoy the game more. I've learned that the more experience I gain completing difficult crossword puzzles, the more I expand my analytical ability to solve complex conundrums.

In these games the goal is to win—to solve the challenge and find the right word—which makes me even more grateful that there's no puzzle to solve when it comes to experiencing the spiritual power of God's Word in our lives. When we live in our anointing in the Spirit, the Word is foundational to our faith. Fueled by the power of God's Word and reliant on the embodiment of Christ as the Word made flesh, we are sustained for victory no matter what we face.

When your anointing is anchored by truth—the Word always wins!

The Power of Word Play

Many doctors, neurologists, psychologists, and medical researchers have concluded that playing word games helps keep our cognitive abilities healthy as we age. The habit of thinking, analyzing, and solving presented by crosswords or Wordle or other language-based pastimes prevent our brains from growing complacent, stagnant, and dull from lack of use. Just as the power of word play facilitates cognitive health, we more than benefit from the power of the Word at play in our lives. Through the Spirit dwelling in us, these Word-given benefits are not merely cognitive but comprehensive, supernatural, and transformative.

Along with the gift of the Holy Spirit, the Word has the power to transform us.

David experienced the power of the Word in his anointing and was in turn anointed to express his life in the Spirit by writing psalms. His work was not simply a creative pastime but part of the long tradition of expressing communication with God through specific forms of language, which reflects the literary genre we know as poetry. The biblical book we call Psalms would have been known in David's time as *tehillim*, a Hebrew title literally meaning "praise songs." The name we use came from the Greek word *psalmoi*, which also translates as "songs of praise."

While David is often regarded as the author of Psalms, this collection of divinely inspired poetry and music existed long before he added to them—likely as far back as the time of Moses. And the collected psalms include poems added after David's lifetime, including psalms composed by David's servant Asaph and son Solomon. Most Bible historians conclude that our book of Psalms reflects a span of approximately a thousand years. But their beauty, truth, and impact transcend time because they reflect timeless aspects of the human condition as well as many eternal promises of God.

In ancient times, psalms often served as lyrics accompanied by music, but not always. Whether set to music or expressed as poetic song, psalms express the full range of human emotions—not just praise, including those feelings that often seem to challenge our faith such as fear, doubt, depression, anxiety, anger, resentment, and grief. The diversity of expression found in the Psalms provides permission, comfort, solace, and instruction for how we continue to rely on God's Word in the midst of daily living. God is never surprised by anything we experience and feel. He invites us to open our hearts to Him and trust that He is always present with us, no matter our circumstances or mood.

Psalms of lament, for example, convey the anguish, sorrow, sadness, and grief of the speaker crying out to God. Psalms of pilgrimage, often labeled as "a song of ascent," provided spiritual insight, instruction, and nourishment for pilgrims traveling to Jerusalem three times a year for the annual Jewish festivals. Psalms of praise offer direct songs of responsive joy, admiration, and appreciation for God's character, His goodness, provision, and protection. Similarly, psalms of thanksgiving expressed gratitude for blessings, safety, sustenance, and deliverance. We also find wisdom psalms providing instruction and royal psalms reflecting both the history of Israel's king as well as prophetically referring to the Messiah.

The Psalms offer a voice for virtually every aspect of human experience and emotion. You don't have to be a poet or musician to appreciate the rich depth of expression they offer for all that you face in life. Whether you're overcoming those who doubt you, slaying a giant, or celebrating God's victory in your life, His Word lives in you and through you just as it did with David. Regardless of the occasion or season of life, God's Word expresses, empowers, and exercises your anointing!

God's Anointing in Action

We certainly see this convergence of David's life, his faith, his anointing, and his growth reflected in his contribution to God's Word. David's psalms, which comprise at least seventy-three and roughly half of our canonical collection, often seem to emerge from his life circumstances and personal experiences. They provide evidence and illustrations of God's anointing in action—both in David's life as well as our own.

Sometimes this autobiographical catalyst is quite clear, such as when Saul sent his men to spy on David's house at night and wait in ambush to kill him in the morning (see 1 Samuel 19:11). David knew they were watching and waiting for him, however, thanks to his wife Michal's warning. He turned his escape into the basis for Psalm 59, in which he declares, "You are my strength, I watch for you; you, God, are my fortress, my God on whom I can rely" (Psalm 59:9–10). Saul's men were watching David in order to kill him in a vulnerable moment. David, however, makes it clear that he was watching God and was secure in the safety of God's fortress-like protection.

When David took refuge from Saul's persecution in Gath, David became afraid that Achish, the king there, was after him as well so he pretended to be a madman in order to survive (see 1 Samuel 21:10–15). Knowing this context reveals David's inspiration in writing Psalm 56, including these poignant and poetic lines:

> Be merciful to me, my God,
> for my enemies are in hot pursuit;
> all day long they press their attack.
> My adversaries pursue me all day long;
> in their pride many are attacking me.
> When I am afraid, I put my trust in you.
> In God, whose word I praise—
> in God I trust and am not afraid.
> What can mere mortals do to me?
> All day long they twist my words;
> all their schemes are for my ruin.
>
> Psalm 56:1–5

Notice how David describes his remedy to the fear he was experiencing. "When I am afraid, I put my trust in you. In God, whose word I praise—in God I trust and am not afraid." David knew he could not prevent himself from feeling fear—there was good reason because his life was in danger. He could, however, choose how he responded to that natural fear—by praising God's Word and putting his trust in the Lord. When we put our trust in God, we rely on the power of His Word in us—which leads us to praise!

The Word with You

In our busy, clamorous, noisy world today, silence is often a soothing gift. We're unfortunately used to being bombarded by a cacophony of voices, live and automated, informing us, instructing us, directing us, provoking us, and demanding our attention. Add in other layers, such as traffic, machinery, music, advertising, and it's no wonder we struggle to focus. Which provides a good reminder of our need to eliminate other voices, noise, and audial, ambient clutter in order to hear the voice of God's Spirit within us.

While we often need stillness and silence in order to spend time with God and grow spiritually, there's another kind of silence that becomes deadly—spiritual silence. When we're not communicating with God, when we're not listening to His voice, when we're not attuned to the whisper of the Holy Spirit, when we're not frequently immersed in the pages of His Word, then the eyes of our heart start to go blind.

No one loves this kind of deadly silence and spiritual blindness more than the devil.

The enemy of your soul despises the Word and wants to silence it in your life.

His objective is not to eliminate your relationships with friends, your focus on finances, or your plans for the future; his objective is much more sinister, subtle, and insidious—to loosen your grip on the Word. The devil wants you Wordless and untethered to God's truth so that he can penetrate your thinking, your attitude, and your actions, undermine your faith, and neutralize your anointing. He will do everything he can and draw on the full power of hell to make you let go of the Word, to drop the Word, to abandon the Word, to dismiss the Word, to forsake the Word.

Hell wants you Wordless!

Why? Because when you have the Word, when you carry the Word, when you pray and declare the Word, all things are possible! When you abide in the living Word, Jesus, and His Word abides in you, then you can ask Him for anything by faith and it will be granted.

Bold? Audacious? Dangerous? Yes—but this is not wishful thinking on my part. Jesus told His followers, "If you remain in me and my words remain in you, ask whatever you wish, and it will be done for you" (John 15:7). Jesus had the authority to say this because He Himself is the Word!

In the beginning of John's gospel, the author does not begin with the genealogy of Jesus prior to describing Christ's birth in Bethlehem as Matthew does. Nor does John begin with the baptism of Jesus by John the Baptist and the start of His public ministry as Mark does. John doesn't open his account of Jesus by providing the historical, political, and religious context we find at the beginning of Luke. The gospel of John begins with a much higher, all-encompassing perspective.

> In the beginning was the Word, and the Word was with God, and the Word was God. He was with God in the beginning. Through him all things were made; without him nothing was made that has been made. In him was life, and that life was the light of all mankind. The light shines in the darkness, and the darkness has not overcome it.
>
> John 1:1–5

In the beginning—the beginning of everything in existence—the Word already existed.

The Word was *with* God.

The Word *was* God.

In the beginning was the Word!

The Word is your starting point, the foundation of your anointing.

You're not beginning your next anointing with a curse.

You're not beginning your next anointing with a burden.

You're not beginning your next anointing with a worry.

Your new season of anointing is not starting with fear, anxiety, or depression.

Your new season of anointing is beginning with *the Word*!

The Word begins everything!

The Word Became Flesh

Not only does everything begin with the Word, but the Word has tangible substance and practical presence in your life. John goes on to explain, "The Word became flesh and made his dwelling among us. We have seen his glory, the glory of the one and only Son, who came from the Father, full of grace and truth" (John 1:14). Jesus became human to pay the price for your sins, a debt you could not pay. He died, and through the power of the Holy Spirit—the same Spirit in you—He returned to life and defeated death forever.

The Word became flesh in Jesus—just as the Word became flesh in you!

Which is why your body is sacred—it's the temple of the Holy Spirit within you.

Your anointing makes your faith incarnational and embodied by the Word.

Your new season of anointing is ignited by the Word, Jesus, inside of you and a word from God's Word upon you. All the more reason the enemy wants you Wordless! If the devil can get you to drift away from the Word, then he can get a foothold into your perspective on everything. He can pull you away from the clarity and light of the Word and dim your viewpoint so that you're more vulnerable to temptation.

This is the same strategy the devil attempted with Jesus. You'll recall that after Jesus was baptized by John the Baptist, and after the Spirit descended like a dove and the Father proclaimed His love and anointing upon His Son, Jesus went into the wilderness. After fasting and praying for forty days, the devil saw what he considered an opportunity.

Knowing that Jesus was mortal and human, Satan realized the vulnerability of Christ coming out of this intentional time of prayer and fasting. His body would be weak and hungry from lack of food. His energy level would be lower due to lack of glucose, which might impede His brain's ability to think and process. His security in His identity might even be a bit shaky in this transition from such a private, personal time into full-time public ministry.

So the devil tempted Jesus three times and targeted each of those areas—without success. In each instance, Jesus responded not with physical weapons of swords and slingshots, not with retaliatory words of deception and falsehoods, and not with mind games of manipulation. Jesus defended Himself against the schemes of the devil by relying on the Word of God. "It is written: 'Man shall not live on bread alone, but on every word that comes from the mouth of God'" (Matthew 4:4).

Jesus quoted Scripture from Deuteronomy in response to the devil (see Deuteronomy 8:3). In fact, in each of His rebuttals to the enemy, Jesus cited truth directly from God's Word. He knew there is no more powerful weapon on earth for overcoming the enemy than the Word.

I worry that even in our anointing, we sometimes lose sight of this truth and the impact it has as our spiritual anchor. You see, the world is full of two types of people. Those with a word, and those without a word. The enemy is fully cognizant of the fact that every great biblically recorded achievement, victory, and exploit began with a word.

With a word, Noah built an ark that saved his family and advanced human civilization.

With a word, Abraham offered his son and discovered a ram stuck in the thicket, igniting faith in God's creation.

With a word, Moses confronted Pharaoh and demanded that he let go of God's people so they could worship.

With a word, Joshua shouted down the walls of Jericho.

With a word, the Israelites occupied the promise.

With a word, Gideon came out of the threshing floor.

With a word, Samuel anointed David, David defeated Goliath, and the glory of God arrived in Jerusalem.

With a word, Peter walked on water.

With a word, Lazarus came out of the tomb, and with a Word, better yet as *the* Word, Jesus died on the cross, shedding His blood and giving us eternal, new, and abundant life!

The Word of God always provides a word for you. "Your word is a lamp for my feet, a light on my path" (Psalm 119:105). God's Word reveals your next step and then your next.

He gives you His Word just as He sent His Son, the Word made flesh, into the world for your sake. In the beginning was the Word. Right now is the Word. Later on will be the Word. The truth of God's Word and Christ as the Word remain outside of chronological time as we experience and record it. The Word is timeless. Jesus said, "Heaven and earth will pass away, but my words will never pass away" (Matthew 24:35).

There's a word over your family.

There's a word over your health.

There's a word over your assignment.

There's a word over your calling.

There's a word over your God-ordained purpose.

There's a word over your children and your children's children.

There is a word over your generation, your city, your state, and your nation.

In the beginning was, is, and will be the Word!

Run with the Word

Not only is there a word from God for you, but He accompanies His word for you.

You cannot separate God from His Word! In the beginning the Word already existed. The Word was with God, and God is with you—so His Word is with you!

No matter how big the giant, how long the road, how weary the battle, or how shameful the sin, you always have the Word. When you are anointed in the Spirit of God, He stays with you. When you are anointed in the Spirit of God, His Word stays with you.

The enemy wants you to doubt this, to falsely believe you can drop the Word, lose the Word, and give up the Word. But you cannot be separated from the Word—because you cannot be separated from God.

You'll recall from our exploration and application of spiritual armor that the sword of the Spirit is the Word of God (see Ephesians 6:17). You cannot lose the Spirit, and you cannot lose the Word! The enemy's only shot of taking you out is to blind you and try to make you feel Wordless—hopeless, defeated, desperate, powerless. While you might experience those feelings momentarily, you still have the Word!

I think about the distinction between a fumble and a tackle in football. Members of the other team charge at you, grab you, attempt to pull you down, hit you, and attempt to strip you of the ball you're carrying before they tackle you to the ground. If they succeed in loosening your grip on the ball so that you release it for them to recover, it's a fumble. If you hold on to the ball when pulled to the ground, it's merely a tackle. They've delayed your progress, but you are still moving downfield toward the endzone where you can score. If they cause you to fumble, though, then they have separated you from the ball and your possession of it. You go on the defense and can no longer score until you get the ball back.

At most, the devil can temporarily tackle you and cause you to stumble and momentarily fall before you get up again. He can temporarily hit you and jar the ball loose and cause you to wonder where the Word went. I'm convinced the enemy doesn't primarily want to tackle you. He wants you to fumble. He wants you to let go of your word. The vast majority of fumbles, around 90 percent, so I've been told, take place because the player is holding the ball in a vulnerable place of his body. I suspect the same is true for us with our Word.

You could either have the Word alongside you, or you could have it in your heart. What determines the position of the Word in your life? Your faith!

The Word Has You

If you have your faith in the periphery, if your faith becomes secondary, if your faith is something only for Sundays or when you're desperate because of circumstances, then you are vulnerable for a fumble.

Whatever is at war in your life, the enemy will attack you there. Whatever is exposed in your life, the enemy will attack. That's why you must be rooted by the Word, in the Word, and with the Word, and carry the Word God has given you for your present mission. You must remain grounded by the power of your anointing. Your going in and your coming out, your words and your thoughts, your relationships and conversations—they must all be under the blood.

Do not hold the Word casually on your side—*hold it in your heart.* "I have hidden your word in my heart that I might not sin against you" (Psalm 119:11). And even when you slip and drop the ball, even when you don't see where it landed, even when you feel blindsided by an unexpected loss, crisis, conflict, or giant, you will still win—because ultimately you can never lose the Word you've been given!

Your anointing ensures that you will recover and score, recover and prosper, recover and flourish!

The enemy can tackle you or even cause you to fumble, but he can never take the ball—the Word—away from you! It's not spiritually possible for you to be robbed of the Word and separated from it permanently.

You can lose a lot in this life, but you cannot lose the Word God has for you.

You can lose your shoes but not your Word. You can lose your shirt but not your Word. You can reach your goal without a shirt and shoes but not without the Word. You may have been hit but you did not let go of the Word. You may have lost something, but you did not let go of the Word. You may have been robbed but you did not let go of the Word. You may have lost your job, your house, your car, your phone, your way home, and your dog, but you did not lose your Word. You may have lost your money, friends, relatives, and some sleep, but I have news for you: There's something the enemy was not able to take, and it was his number one objective. That was your God-given Word!

You still have it! You still have the Word and the Word still has you!

We're told, "Faith comes from hearing the message, and the message is heard through the word about Christ" (Romans 10:17). No matter what you've suffered, endured, experienced, survived, or been through—you still have the word of your anointing from the Word of God.

I dare you to declare that after all you've been through, you still have the Word. After all you've survived, you still have the Word! After all you've endured, you still have the Word! After the storm, after the fire, after the valley, after the enemy trying his best to rob, kill and destroy—you still have the Word and know with absolute certainty that the Word has you!

The more you study the Word, the more you read the Word, the more you meditate on the Word, the more you speak the Word, the more you declare the Word, the more you live the Word—the more the Word bears fruit in, with, for, and through you!

The Word of God will never fail.

The Word of God is in you!

Selecting Your Stone

As you consider what it means for you to run with God's Word and experience the full impact of Christ's truth in your life, use these questions as a way to reflect and apply this chapter's main ideas. Consider how God's Spirit has been communicating with you recently, what you've noticed and heard, or what you've been experiencing through the power of the Word. After answering these questions, remove all distractions and spend a few minutes—at least five if not longer—simply listening in your heart for the Spirit's voice.

1. What are some ways you're currently aware of the power of God's Word in your life? What verses or passages in Scripture continue to speak to your heart?

2. When have you fumbled the word God has for you and momentarily faltered in your faith? How did you recover and realize that you can never lose the Word within you?

3. What word or words has God spoken to you most recently? How does this word from the Lord cast a vision for this new season of your anointing in His Spirit?

Dear God, the power and truth of Your Word in my life continues to strengthen me in so many ways. Thank You for the gift of Jesus, the Word made flesh, and for His sacrifice on the cross to pay the debt for my sins. Thank You for the Holy Spirit abiding in me, giving me guidance and instruction, comfort and compassion, friendship and faithfulness. Let me throw off every encumbrance that would hold me back and run in the power of the Word! Give me ears to hear and eyes to see the word You have for me, Lord, as I pursue the fulfillment of Your calling on my life. In Jesus' name, Amen.

FOURTH STONE

INFLUENCE

Anointed to Slay Your Giants with Victory

For everyone born of God overcomes the world. This is the victory that has overcome the world, even our faith. Who is it that overcomes the world? Only the one who believes that Jesus is the Son of God.

1 John 5:4–5

10

Anointed by the Same Spirit

Growing in the Fullness of Resurrection Power

When God's timing reveals itself, you will be ready for your next anointing. You can wait patiently trusting that you are growing from strength to strength!

Among the many joys of being a grandparent, the blessing of seeing the world through the eyes of my grandchildren is one of my favorites. The discovery, surprise, and wonder with which little ones engage the world in the present moment helps me to practice childlike trust in my relationship with God. I'm reminded of when the disciples asked Jesus who should be considered the greatest in the Kingdom of heaven, and He answered, "Truly I tell you, unless you change and become like little children, you will never enter the kingdom of heaven" (Matthew 18:3).

The way kids see even the simplest things not only brings my attention back to details I might overlook but helps me consider them anew—the many "flavors" of green each spring, the way the ocean smells like a "salty goldfish," and the "silly chatter" of birdsong. While these are often unexpected and even humorous, one such observation from my youngest grandson recently caught my attention for its simple yet profound spiritual insight.

We were outside playing in our backyard one late spring morning, when my grandson, then ten years old, became fascinated by the flowerbed and shrubbery my wife had just planted a couple weeks prior. Apparently, he had learned in school to distinguish between plants that were perennials and ones considered annuals and loved showing off his knowledge.

"These are annuals," he said, pointing to some bright red zinnias and yellow marigolds. "They'll die by fall and be done." He then rushed to another spot, knelt by some tulips and irises, and said, "But these are perennials—I remember them from last year! They keep coming back even when you think they're dead." He looked closer at them and lightly touched the soft pink petal of a tulip before announcing, "They're like resurrection flowers!"

I smiled at his clever insight. "You're right! They *are* like resurrection flowers."

We continued our conversation before moving on to kick the soccer ball around, but his comment lingered. It not only made me see tulips and perennials from a fresh perspective but also led me to consider how many times we assume something in our lives has died, when really it's simply waiting to come back to life at the appropriate time.

I fear we live out our anointing this way too often.

We see a dream take root and begin to grow, but then it seems to wither in the next season of our lives. We assume it's dead, that it wasn't meant to be, that we didn't water and tend it properly. We lose sight of the fact that if it's a God-given dream, part of our anointed mission in this life, then it will not die. It might go underground for a season or two, but it's waiting to spring to life—just like my grandson's resurrection flowers!

When you live in the power of the Holy Spirit, you are anointed to flourish. You are anointed with resurrection power. The same Spirit who raised Jesus from the grave resides in you and will restore your dreams with new life.

Nourish to Flourish

While perennials return year after year, we don't usually see how deep their roots are growing. Over the years, we may notice that the hydrangea seems larger and produces more blossoms each spring, but the changes are usually slow and subtle. We don't see its roots extending deeper beneath the ground. We don't witness what's taking place during the in-between seasons that nourish its growth in order for it to flourish.

Our growth from anointing to anointing often happens the same way. We don't realize how God is preparing, equipping, and nourishing us during the interval leading to the fulfillment of our next anointing. Sometimes we may experience rapid growing pains, but most of the time we develop gradually according to God's timing.

David started this process after his first anointing. He was anointed by Samuel as God's chosen, revealing David's character and establishing his identity as the divinely selected next king of Israel. And then he had to wait. Knowing that God had chosen him to be king, David must have experienced an ever-shifting mixture of emotions: excitement, anticipation, fear, uncertainty, confidence, affirmation, anxiety—and definitely impatience.

How long did David wait until he was anointed as king over Judah? We don't know exactly, but it was definitely an extended period of years. While we're not told David's age at his first anointing, we do know he was the youngest of a large family and not old enough yet to enlist in the king's army with his three oldest brothers. The age of conscription and enlistment at that time was usually twenty, so it seems likely that David might have been around fifteen or sixteen years old when Samuel came to Jesse's house and anointed David with oil as Israel's next king.

We're told that after Saul dies and David is anointed king of Judah, he was thirty years old (see 2 Samuel 5:4), which means David waited roughly fifteen years from his first anointing to his next. Think for a moment about how much you changed and developed from the time you were fifteen until you were thirty. During this time of transition, you likely discovered a greater sense of identity and an awareness of your values, beliefs, and faith convictions. You encountered the challenges and responsibilities that come with "adulting." You probably related to people differently as well, testing your ability to trust, commit, and love.

Regardless of the number of years, most people develop and mature in significant ways from adolescence into adulthood, and David was no exception. And for much of this period of waiting, he lived in an ongoing state of uncertainty, at least circumstantially.

Most of this uncertainty resulted from the man David would eventually replace, Saul. Instead of being a mentor eager to teach and prepare his successor, Saul became a teacher of another kind, the center of chaos for this waiting period. You'll recall how David's fame, shortly after defeating Goliath, became a trigger for Saul's insecurity and narcissism. Afraid as well as envious of David's victories in battle and growing popularity, Saul tried to kill David repeatedly and became obsessed with eliminating this young man who proceeded to be everything Saul was not.

In order to survive the king and his assassins, David had to flee and go into hiding, constantly vigilant in order to stay alive. This time on the run as a fugitive, however, only reinforced and honed David's character and the qualities he would need to unite and rule over all twelve tribes of Israel. Traits such as resourcefulness, resilience, courage, loyalty, and leadership. David learned how to trust and love others, including his spiritual brother Jonathan, Saul's son and presumed heir, and his wife Michal, Saul's daughter.

Despite having committed no crime and, in fact, achieved success for the very man determined to kill him, David never doubted God's presence in his life. Forced to be a fugitive when he had been chosen to be king, David could have doubted God's promise and become angry, resentful, and bitter—ironically, all the traits we see in Saul. Instead, David remained patient and trusted in God's timing, confidently declaring, "I remain confident of this: I will see the goodness of the LORD in the land of the living" (Psalm 27:13). And what would he do until then? "Wait for the LORD; be strong and take heart and wait for the LORD" (Psalm 27:14).

As you grow toward your next anointing, you are invited to do the same.

To be strong.

To take heart.

To wait for the Lord.

Flexing Your Faith

Waiting is rarely easy—especially when it involves delayed gratification, which it often does. Our vast technological advancements, as wonderfully efficient and mechanically miraculous as they are, have conditioned us to want, click, and receive. We have the ability to connect, communicate, consume, and conduct commerce online anytime day or night. If someone hasn't responded to our text right away, we fear they're ghosting us. If the package doesn't arrive next day, assuming same day isn't possible, then we can't understand the delay.

Patience, which was historically regarded as a moral virtue, has become little more than an indicator of customer satisfaction. If we have to wait more than five minutes to get our food after ordering—three if we're in the drive-thru—then we're frustrated and wonder what's taking so long. Simply put, we consistently expect the amount of time in between our catalyst and our conclusion to be shorter and shorter. We want results, satisfaction, our order, our payment, our pain relief, our reservation, our ticket, our seat, our opportunity, our big break—and we want them all now.

Spiritual growth, however, requires patience—more patience than we think we have. But fortunately, our patience relies on the Holy Spirit within us and not our own human capacity for waiting. Scripture frequently urges us not only to be patient but to cultivate patience for its benefits. The way James explains this counterintuitive process reminds me of the way our body's muscles grow when we exercise:

> When troubles of any kind come your way, consider it an opportunity for great joy. For you know that when your faith is tested, your endurance has a chance to grow. So let it grow, for when your endurance is fully developed, you will be perfect and complete, needing nothing.
>
> James 1:2–4

Resistance training, usually involving weights or dumbbells, stresses our muscles from the exertion of our exercise. Tissue breaks down—think about pushing yourself until your arms shake from fatigue—and grows back stronger as a result. Similarly, endurance athletes test their body's limits by increasing the time and distance they cover during workouts and competitions. Someone doesn't wake up one day and decide to enter the Ironman Triathlon. They begin slowly with short distances that may take them a while at first and gradually grow into covering longer distances faster.

Your faith works the same way when you're waiting on your next anointing. Instead of grumbling, stumbling, or fumbling when troubles of any kind come your way, you can use them as opportunities for flexing your faith. When you flex your faith, your endurance has a chance to grow. The original Greek word translated as "endurance" is *hupomoné*, which conveys an active perseverance, steadfastness, and patience. This kind of endurance isn't passively waiting around like a victim of circumstance, worrying and fretting into powerlessness and despair. No, the kind of endurance James talks about, which we see throughout the Bible, is the kind that's expectant, anticipatory, confident, and steady.

As your endurance has a chance to grow, it blossoms with patience. When your endurance is fully developed, mature, and complete, you will bear the tension of trials and the stress of unexpected struggles without needing anything else.

You won't need a distraction, a diversion, or a disruption because you know that God is in control and right on time. You won't need a substance to elevate or depress your mood and mindset because you can relax in your anointing with the peace that passes understanding. You won't need a calendar, stopwatch, alarm clock, timer, or snooze button to remind you how long you must wait because God will tell you the right time with eternal precision.

And what will He tell you?

In the course of time, God will tell you, "Go up."

Grow Up to Go Up

When God's timing reveals itself, you will be ready for your next anointing. When you *grow up*, God will tell you to *go up*! This is what we see in the example of David when his wait was finally over. At first glance we might assume the catalyst for David's second anointing and ascension to the throne is the death of King Saul, which is described in detail in the final book of 1 Samuel. And it's worth noting that Saul's death is not quick, easy, or painless—just the opposite, it seems.

Israel had continued to battle the relentless Philistines throughout Saul's reign, and the king's final stand near Mount Gilboa was particularly brutal. Not only were many slaughtered on the mountain's slopes, but the Philistines killed three of Saul's sons, including David's beloved friend Jonathan. Facing his own imminent death, Saul even asked his armor bearer to use his sword and kill him quickly before the pagan enemies attacked, which the frightened soldier refused to do. Seeing no other way, Saul fell on his own sword and died.

While many soldiers, commanders, and kings throughout history have taken their own lives rather than die at the hands of bloodthirsty enemies, Saul's choice resonates with the weight of someone who continually relied on himself instead of God. The Spirit had departed from Saul many years earlier, leaving the king to experience the consequences of living in his own limitations. Samuel had even warned Saul:

> You have done a foolish thing. . . . You have not kept the command the LORD your God gave you; if you had, he would have established your kingdom over Israel for all time. But now your kingdom will not endure; the LORD has sought out a man after his own heart and appointed him ruler of his people, because you have not kept the LORD's command.
>
> 1 Samuel 13:13–14

When faced with impossible odds of surviving, Saul used his weapon to slay himself.

When faced with impossible odds of surviving, David used his weapon to slay a giant.

The difference influencing their choices and actions came down to their relationship with God. Saul refused to continue trusting God, in part because he grew impatient with God's timing and methods. David couldn't imagine not trusting God, knowing full well what his vulnerabilities and limitations were. David accepted and embraced God's

Spirit at work in him to do what he could not do on his own—in killing Goliath to do what no one else could do.

Once Saul had finally died, it would seem that David's time had finally come. But David didn't immediately rush his accession to the throne. Historically, upon the death of a ruling monarch, his heir or successor was immediately crowned as the new king or queen. While the new ruler's public coronation typically occurs later, leaders feared allowing time to pass—time that might be exploited by enemies or others with royal aspirations. This tradition has endured for centuries and continues even now. When Queen Elizabeth II died in 2022, for example, her oldest son inherited the monarchy and became King Charles III on the same day that she passed. His coronation, however, did not occur until the following May of 2023.

The moment Saul died, however, David was not immediately king. David continued to wait on God before assuming his next anointing.

In the Course of Time

After learning of Saul's death and the loss of his spiritual brother Jonathan, David mourned and grieved both of them. It would be understandable after waiting nearly fifteen years if David had decided—personally, politically, strategically—that he had better seize this opportunity he had spent half his life waiting to happen and declare himself king. Instead, David continued to rely on God's timing:

> In the course of time, David inquired of the LORD. "Shall I go up to one of the towns of Judah?" he asked.
>
> The LORD said, "Go up."
>
> David asked, "Where shall I go?"
>
> "To Hebron," the LORD answered.
>
> So David went up there with his two wives, Ahinoam of Jezreel and Abigail, the widow of Nabal of Carmel. David also took the men who were with him, each with his family, and they settled in Hebron and its towns. Then the men of Judah came to Hebron, and there they anointed David king over the tribe of Judah.
>
> 2 Samuel 2:1–4

Anything strike you about how David's royal anointing goes down? It's so indirect and roundabout that it's almost comical by today's power-grabbing standards! We're told, "In the course of time," which encompasses more waiting, more patience, more endurance and anticipation. Rather than ask God, as you or I might be inclined, "Is it time yet? Saul's dead so I'm thinking now's my time, right? Where's the anointing oil and my crown?"

But that's not what happens. Instead, David simply asks God without any indication of entitlement or expectation, "Should I move closer to Judah?" I love how David's humility persists here rather than any hint of self-absorbed pride or greed for power. David is willing to take action—to move forward—but he's not forcing his way onto the throne just yet.

And what does God tell him? "Go up."

David wants a more specific location, so God directs him to Hebron.

It's almost as if God is waiting on David to inquire before instructing him where to go.

I suspect this is often the case with us as well. We've been anointed and waiting patiently, hiding out in the wilderness of life, slaying the giants of our generation, dealing with complicated relationships, wondering when it will be time for our next anointing. All the while, God may actually be waiting on us! We're waiting around in the course of time, and God's waiting on us and knowing, "Of course it's time!"

While I encourage you wholeheartedly to wait on God, to cultivate patience, to count it all joy when your experience trials that can strengthen your faith and endurance, I also encourage you to be ready for your next anointing right now!

When God tells you to go up, you want to be listening.

When God tells you to go up, you will be ready for your next anointing.

You will be ready for more of the Spirit's power in your life.

You will be ready for more responsibility, more authority, and more leadership.

You will be ready for more abundant blessings.

You will be ready for more influence to ignite change.

You will be ready to prove hell wrong.

You will be ready to slay your giants!

From Strength to Strength

David's second anointing at Hebron made him king of Judah, not over all of Israel just yet. While he only ruled one tribe and not all twelve, this transition allowed David time to acclimate to new responsibilities of leadership. David reigned over Judah for seven and a half years, a tumultuous time of transition after the death of Saul. Because even though the previous king had died, his loyalists and family members continued to jockey for power among the nation's twelve tribes. "The war between the house of Saul and the house of David lasted a long time. David grew stronger and stronger, while the house of Saul grew weaker and weaker" (2 Samuel 3:1).

Even when Saul's son Ish-Bosheth became king, those in Judah—and likely in scattered pockets of the other tribes—remained loyal to David. Attempting to stabilize his shaky power base, Ish-Bosheth ruled only two years before he was murdered by two of his own men, officers of his army who killed him as he slept one night. They audaciously assumed they would be rewarded when they went before David and held up the head of Ish-Bosheth. Instead, David condemned their treachery and had them executed (see 2 Samuel 4:1–12).

In the fallout of their king's assassination, the other tribes of Israel realized they had few options and remained vulnerable to the Philistines and other enemies. David was the obvious choice, a proven leader chosen by God, so they swallowed their pride and arranged to meet.

> All the tribes of Israel came to David at Hebron and said, "We are your own flesh and blood. In the past, while Saul was king over us, you were the one who led Israel on their military campaigns. And the LORD said to you, 'You will shepherd my people Israel, and you will become their ruler.'"
>
> When all the elders of Israel had come to King David at Hebron, the king made a covenant with them at Hebron before the LORD, and they anointed David king over Israel.
>
> David was thirty years old when he became king, and he reigned forty years. In Hebron he reigned over Judah seven years and six months, and in Jerusalem he reigned over all Israel and Judah thirty-three years.
>
> 2 Samuel 5:1–5

Finally, after waiting more than twenty years, David received his third anointing and the fulfillment of his first when God chose him as Israel's king. Notice that not only did the leaders of the Jewish tribes acknowledge the kinship and blood ties they shared with David, but more importantly, they recognized God's anointing of him as their king. David made a covenant with them and agreed to be their royal shepherd, a servant leader who would unite God's people and restore Jerusalem.

Throughout the entire journey to his third anointing, David waited with supernatural patience thanks to God's Spirit empowering him from within. Rather than putting his life on hold or becoming entitled because of his future position, David remained present to learn, grow, and mature day by day, from strength to strength. "Blessed are those whose strength is in you. . . . They go from strength to strength, till each appears before God in Zion" (Psalm 84:5–7). David endured the process required for the fulfillment of his anointing, in stark contrast to Saul who disobeyed God and followed his own royal whims.

When you are faithful and wait on God's timing, He will sustain you with what you need to grow. Like the psalmist, when you place your strength in the Lord, you flex and grow your capacity as a Spirit-led steward for more.

Trust that you will see God's goodness in this life.

Trust that you are being prepared for the fulfillment of your anointing.

Trust that a new season of your anointing is about to begin!

Selecting Your Stone

As you move from strength to strength and overcome all obstacles in your path, pause for a moment to consider how far God has already brought you. Reflect on the impact of your anointings by using the questions below to help enhance your appreciation of the Holy Spirit's unlimited power and divine guidance in your life. Quiet yourself before God with gratitude and spend a few moments listening for the whisper of God's Spirit in your heart. Pay attention to any promptings and don't be surprised if you sense God telling you that it's time to "go up"!

1. What have you seen God do in your life since your first anointing in the power of the Holy Spirit? How has He led you from strength to strength?

2. How has your faith grown because of all you've endured during times of trouble? What spiritual muscles have developed to make you a stronger, more effective leader for those around you?

3. On a scale of 1 to 10, with 1 being "as impatient as a toddler" and 10 being "as patient as a saint," how would you score yourself at present? What in particular are you waiting for as you anticipate your next anointing?

Dear God, forgive me for those times when I get so impatient and try to take matters in my own hands rather than trust Your Spirit within me. Remind me that nothing is wasted—no time, no experience, no relationships—in Your divine economy as I grow and mature into the fulfillment of my next anointing. Grant me supernatural peace and patience to go at Your pace and not my own or anyone else's. Thank You for the season ahead and all that You have for me in my next anointed position of stewardship. In Jesus' name, Amen.

11

Giants Are Slain in the Valley

Forging Influence in Adversity

Anointed by the Holy Spirit, you abide in the Good Shepherd's presence, protection, and provision. No matter how dark your valley or how big your giant, you have everything you need!

Every pilgrimage of faith includes some blisters.

This observation came from a friend who had recently completed walking the Camino de Santiago, also known as the Way of St. James, with a group of other pilgrims from his church. My friend explained how there are numerous ways to complete the network of trails, roads, and paths depending on your starting point but that all of them culminate at the cathedral in Santiago de Compostela, located in northwestern Spain.

Historically, one of the most frequently chosen starting points remains Saint-Jean-de-Port in France, a route spanning nearly five hundred miles and requiring four to six weeks to complete on foot. My friend and his group chose a more beginner-friendly route starting in Sarria, Spain, roughly seventy miles away from their final destination. In addition to travel time for arrival and departure, they budgeted seven days for the actual pilgrimage, requiring they trek about ten miles per day.

My friend is the first to confess that he's not in prime athletic shape, so the physical toll of hiking ten miles a day for a week with a backpack weighing over twenty pounds definitely presented a barrier. The trail followed the sloping terrain of northern Spain, resulting in plenty of uphill stretches before winding into more gentle valleys of descent. Each day presented its own challenges: unseasonably hot temperatures one day, a sudden thunderstorm the next, nausea from exotic foods, and just the sheer fatigue from poor sleep in hostels, inns, and tents along the Way.

The most enjoyable aspect of this pilgrimage according to my friend was the diversity of other pilgrims. He had expected most participants to be Christians from either the United States or nearby European countries such as France and Portugal. Instead, pilgrims reflected virtually every demographic imaginable—including age, ethnicity, education level, income, and religion. My friend met Muslim teens, Jewish seniors, and an agnostic family with young children. Some pilgrims approached their course each day like a marathon while others enjoyed a more leisurely pace, some with the latest hiking gear available online and others with well-worn, dirty boots and packs from frequent use. Many were in groups, others in families, and a good number were on their own.

Based on conversations had and overheard by my friend, each pilgrim seemed to have set an intention for their journey on the Camino. One Australian couple was considering marriage, a young Italian woman was contemplating whether to finalize her vows as a Dominican nun, and an elderly Irishman admitted he was thinking about his own mortality, grateful to be completing this bucket item on his list. Several people my friend talked with along the Way were in recovery from an addiction, seeking clarity and perspective on their new sober season of life. Others were there to assess their faith and how they relate to God, to pray and draw closer to Christ. But almost everyone had something they chose to face during their completion of this ancient pilgrimage dating back centuries.

They knew that in order to overcome their giant, they had to go through the valley.

They chose to confront the obstacles before them and keep walking.

They understood what we, too, experience as we grow in our anointings. Regardless of the topography of our locale, giants are slain in the valleys.

Pinnacle of Purpose

Perhaps I will undertake a pilgrimage along the Camino de Santiago someday myself, but in the meantime, I'm grateful for the power to slay life's giants no matter where I am. Because we all face them just like David in his showdown with Goliath. But as David also learned on his way to be anointed king over all of Israel, giants can come in all shapes and sizes.

King Saul with his murderous fear, anger, and jealousy toward David became even more dangerous in many ways than the Philistine giant. Goliath, for all his alpha swagger and giant-sized intimidation, fell with only one stone. Saul continued to threaten, harass, and stalk David for more than a decade, right up until Saul's death.

Other than his complex relationship with Saul, David also battled giant struggles within himself, as we all do. Human beings inevitably face internal conflicts as they experience big emotions such as anger, fear, and lust—which in turn can lead to violence, addiction, and deception. While David mostly seems to have won this battle and maintained a positive attitude within himself, ultimately, he was not immune.

His internal giant manifested during a seemingly peaceful time. After his third anointing, David was finally king over all of Israel. He had restored Jerusalem as the capital of Israel—making it forever the "City of David"—and returned the Ark of the Covenant to the temple there. He was renowned and revered as a courageous warrior and leader of the nation's armies. He lived in a splendid royal palace with his wives and children. What could go wrong?

> In the spring, at the time when kings go off to war, David sent Joab out with the king's men and the whole Israelite army. They destroyed the Ammonites and besieged Rabbah. But David remained in Jerusalem.

> One evening David got up from his bed and walked around on the roof of the palace. From the roof he saw a woman bathing. The woman was very beautiful, and David sent someone to find out about her. The man said, "She is Bathsheba, the daughter of Eliam and the wife of Uriah the Hittite." Then David sent messengers to get her. She came to him, and he slept with her. (Now she was purifying herself from her monthly uncleanness.) Then she went back home. The woman conceived and sent word to David, saying, "I am pregnant."
>
> 2 Samuel 11:1–5

What could have prompted David's choice to send for another man's wife whom he spied bathing from his palace rooftop one sleepless evening? You don't have to be a psychologist to see that David doesn't fall into this situation merely because of lust—complacency seems to be a factor as well. What time of year is it? Spring. And what usually happens each spring? Kings go off to war. Where is King David? He remained in Jerusalem. Why? We don't know exactly.

It's easy to speculate on why David stayed behind and sent Joab out with the entire army of Israel without himself, their king, to lead them. Perhaps David was getting older and growing weary of life on the battlefield. Instead of roughing it outdoors in a military camp, David could remain safe and comfortable in his palace in Jerusalem. Maybe he felt that he had nothing left to prove because of his lifetime success as a warrior and leader of victorious battles over the Philistines. Or, I suspect, David might have reached a point in midlife when he questioned what the rest of his life would hold. With his third anointing, he had seen the fulfillment of God's calling on his life.

David had reached the pinnacle of his purpose.

He had defeated Goliath, eluded Saul's madness and murderous mayhem, united all twelve tribes of Israel, restored Jerusalem, returned the Ark of the Covenant, married multiple women, and fathered numerous children. We know by this time David had been a shepherd, an armor bearer, a giant-slayer, a soldier, a musician, and a poet. He had single-handedly killed thousands of men and led his army to conquer thousands more. And most importantly David was a man after God's own heart.

But David was still human.

Still a man.

Still vulnerable to unexpected giants within himself.

From Wondering to Wandering

Regardless of the context and motive for David's decision to remain in Jerusalem that spring, he made a choice to stay behind. To do things differently that year rather than the usual go-to-war because it's spring again. Boredom, complacency, irresponsibility, depression, insecurity—perhaps none or even all of those and more factored into his decision.

When we experience the fullness of our anointing, we inevitably face a similar choice.

When we reach the pinnacle of our purpose, we don't realize how vulnerable we are.

When we climb the summit after years of dedication, we expose our weaknesses.

We can continue doing what we've always done and leading the way that got us to where we are. Or we can coast a little. Stay behind and take some time for ourselves. Enjoy the fruits of our labor and the many blessings God has bestowed in our lives. Having reached this pinnacle, we wonder what's left to accomplish, attain, and achieve. We wonder if life is all downhill from here. So rather than remain faithful to the holy habits and faithful lifestyle that got us to the top, we decide to take some time to enjoy ourselves and to figure out why we're so restless and resistant. Such reflection and introspection can be tremendously helpful and rejuvenating, just as observing Sabbath rest is essential for recharging and renewing our connection with God.

But David didn't use his time at home for any of these endeavors.

Instead, David couldn't sleep and got up to wander around.

David wandered up to the palace rooftop, where his eyes wandered to the scene below him: a very beautiful woman bathing. He asked around and found out her name. He sent for her. She came to him and they slept together. She went home and then informed David she was pregnant with his child.

It almost seems as if David's tendency to wander physically leads to wandering spiritually as well. Because not only was it his feet and his eyes that wandered—it was also his heart. His heart wandered as his mind wondered what was left for him. Having reached the pinnacle of his purpose, David seems to have wandered from his power source.

Perhaps you've heard the saying, "Power tends to corrupt, and absolute power corrupts absolutely." It's credited to a nineteenth-century British historian, Lord Acton, and refers to our human tendency to allow power to inflate our egos into entitlement to the point of addictive reliance. We begin to define ourselves by the privileges of power to the point that we will do whatever we deem necessary to hold on to both. The more power, the higher the stakes—and the greater the treachery to maintain it.

While David knew that everything he had accomplished across his entire life resulted from the power of God's Spirit in him, he seems to have disconnected from his awareness of that truth one spring evening in Jerusalem on a palace rooftop. Perhaps it was the thrill of Bathsheba's beauty and the desire to be fulfilled by her. Perhaps it was the challenge of her being another man's wife and seemingly unattainable. Perhaps it was the lustful arousal of a very beautiful woman leading to pleasure that could make him feel young again.

Whatever it was, it was not of God.

It was a giant requiring a different strategic stone.

Your Heart, God's Spirit

The consequences of David's adultery with Bathsheba unraveled his life and the lives of so many others both directly and indirectly. The events might seem like tropes from a contemporary soap opera if not for their tragic reality: scheming to cover up his affair, ordering the death of her husband, suffering the death of their infant son, learning his daughter was raped by his son, discovering another son murdered his half-brother in vengeance, and battling that same son who incited a civil war against David.

Despite all of these consequences and the severity of their impact, David found a way to slay the giant within him—with some help from the prophet Nathan. God was displeased with David, and I'm guessing disappointed as well, but He did not abandon His anointed king. Instead, God sent Nathan to confront David, and knowing the resistance, denial, and anger he would face before the king, Nathan employed a brilliant strategy. Rather than confront David's sin of adultery and murder directly, Nathan told David a parable that objectified David's crimes enough for him to see the horrific injustice he had perpetrated. The strategy worked and David repented, fully aware there would be devastating consequences.

During his repentance, David wrote one of the most powerful and personal psalms in the Bible, Psalm 51. It remains a timeless template for confessing our sins to God and asking for His mercy, compassion, and forgiveness. Throughout the psalm, David focuses on how he has sinned foremost against God—by not obeying and trusting the power of God's Spirit within him. With humility, sincerity, and an earnest desire for restoration, David brings it back to a matter of his heart and the Holy Spirit:

> Create in me a pure heart, O God,
> and renew a steadfast spirit within me.
> Do not cast me from your presence
> or take your Holy Spirit from me.
> Restore to me the joy of your salvation
> and grant me a willing spirit, to sustain me.
>
> You do not delight in sacrifice, or I would bring it;
> you do not take pleasure in burnt offerings.
> My sacrifice, O God, is a broken spirit;
> a broken and contrite heart
> you, God, will not despise.
>
> Psalm 51:10–12, 16–17

David prays that God will not abandon him or take the Holy Spirit from within him. He asks for a pure heart and a steadfast spirit—one that endures and patiently perseveres. He offers his heart, broken and repentant, as his only sacrifice. David's prayer here illustrates another dimension of why he was considered a man after God's own heart. David relied on God's Spirit within him and the power of his anointing—and when he failed, he humbly confessed, asked for forgiveness, embraced repentant restoration, and got back on his feet.

God forgave David and ultimately blessed him with being a forerunner and forebearer of His Son, Jesus Christ. David is listed among the lineage of patriarchs in the genealogy of Jesus in Matthew's gospel—which also mentions, surprisingly enough, Bathsheba, although she is referred to as the wife of Uriah (see Matthew 1:6). It's striking that even though their relationship began with adultery and resulted in death and devastation for many family members, ultimately they are recognized for their anointing as God's chosen.

David's sin with Bathsheba reminds us both of what *not* to do—wander from God—as well as what to do when we stumble and fall—repent wholeheartedly. Confess our sins before God and focus on what David reminds us to focus on: our heart and God's Spirit.

Spiritual and Cultural Giants

While it's easy to look across the pages of our Bibles and the facts of history to see David's giants, it can be challenging to recognize our own. Like David, we are facing giants—intimidating, overwhelming forces designed to keep us from fulfilling our divine calling. Today's giants, however, are not physical warriors ten feet tall but spiritual and cultural giants determined to take us out. These are enemies, obstacles, conflicts, challenges, and struggles that arise in our lives almost every day in some form, including:

Complacency: The idea that "good enough" is acceptable, leading to stagnation.

Conformity: The pressure to blend in rather than stand out as ambassadors of the Kingdom.

Comfortability: The refusal to embrace discomfort, which is often the seedbed of growth.

Moral relativism: A culture where truth is subjective and personal preferences outweigh biblical standards.

Cultural decadence: The normalization of sin and the celebration of what the Bible calls evil.

Spiritual apathy: A Church asleep, unwilling to engage in battle for souls.

Ecclesiastical lukewarmness: Ministries that value popularity over prophetic truth.

Perpetual victimization modalities: A society obsessed with offense and entitlement rather than victory and responsibility.

Toxic atmospheres: Environments that suffocate faith and breed division.

Spiritual promiscuity: A generation that chases spiritual experiences without biblical foundation.

Giants of nonsense: A war against common sense, logic, and biblical wisdom.

If we fail to recognize this battle, we risk being silenced, sidelined, and spiritually suffocated. Romans 12:2 warns us, "Do not conform to the pattern of this world, but be transformed by the renewing of your mind." At the core of this conflict is a battle between two realms—one dictated by fear, confusion, and compromise, and the other by faith, clarity, and conviction. This battle is between:

Our mind and our mantle: Will we align with worldly thinking or God's calling?

Anointing and ambition: Will we chase platforms or pursue the presence of God?

Fear and faith: Will we shrink back or step forward?

The pathetic and the prophetic: Will we live in mediocrity or move in divine authority?

Light and darkness: A battle as old as time, but increasingly evident in today's world.

Our past and our future: Will we remain stuck in yesterday or step into our divine destiny?

Our memories and our imagination: Will we be limited by past failures or envision a future shaped by faith?

Common sense and nonsense: Will we hold to biblical truth or be deceived by cultural chaos?

Feelings and faith: Will we be led by emotions or by God's promises?

Opinions and facts: Will we be swayed by popular belief or anchored in biblical truth?

Making history or making excuses: Will we advance the Kingdom or explain away our inaction?

This is the battle we cannot afford to lose. And thanks be to God, we don't have to!

The Lord Is Your Shepherd

Often these contemporary giants looming around us and testing our faith can release their internal twins in our minds, hearts, and spirits. Because so often, how we handle the external giants either sets free our internal giants of fear, anxiety, depression, rage, lust, greed, and addiction—or shrinks them down to size. When we remain in the power of our anointing in the Spirit, when we hold steadfast to our faith and refuse to allow ourselves to wander, then we slay our giants before they can rise out of the valleys where we encounter them.

But there will be dark valleys to traverse and giants, both loud and obvious as well as quiet and subtle, across the span of your life. You will encounter betrayals you could never have imagined from those you know and trust. You will experience losses that overwhelm you with sorrow, grief, anger, and overwhelming pain. You will expect something—a job offer, a marriage proposal, a promised bonus—that will inevitably leave you disappointed.

In those moments, darkness will close in around you and limit your vision. You will lack the strength to get back on your feet and you may wonder how God could have allowed this to happen. You will feel overwhelmed by confusion, uncertainty, and doubt as the bedrock foundation of your faith gets shaken.

During those dark times, unexpected giants often rise up in hopes of slaying you in your weakness. The enemy knows our vulnerabilities and seizes every opportunity to undermine our faith and draw us away from the knowledge, power, and purpose of our anointing. Natural coping mechanisms to reduce pain and seek pleasure suddenly lead us into traps of shameful addictions, perpetual victimization, unrestrained hedonism, moral relativism, theological promiscuity, and spiritual wounding.

You didn't see these giants coming because you were surrounded by darkness in the valley. But suddenly there they are, and your confidence wavers because you feel weary, beaten, and bruised. You can't find the energy to defend yourself, let alone attack the giants intent on your destruction.

This is when you must call on the name of the Lord and allow Him to protect you, to provide for you, and to hold you close within the presence of His Spirit as comforter and friend. This is when you must allow God's Word to be a light unto your path and show you the way out of the dark valley. This is when you must claim the valley promise as uttered and written, inspired by the Holy Spirit, by the same David who went through valleys and faced giants before you. "Even when I walk through the darkest valley, I will not be afraid, for you are close beside me. Your rod and your staff protect and comfort me" (Psalm 23:4 NLT).

The Lord is your shepherd. And He never abandons His sheep.

Anointed in the power of the Holy Spirit, you're attuned to the Good Shepherd's presence, protection, and provision. No matter how dark your valley or how big your giant, you have everything you need to persevere. Trusting in the power of God's Spirit within you—the same Spirit resurrecting Jesus from the tomb—you can slay every giant and emerge from every valley. As others notice your integrity, your influence will increase.

The giants you slay in your valleys enable you to climb higher in your influence.

What you fight in your private valleys enables you to be victorious in your public mountaintops. Your anointing empowers you with whatever spiritual stones you need to conquer those internal struggles and to fortify yourself against the enemy's temptations and snares.

Even in the darkest valleys, you will overcome every giant.

Jesus, the Good Shepherd, is close beside you every step of the way.

His rod and His staff comfort you.

You don't need to be afraid.

Giants are slain in the valley!

Selecting Your Stone

While it can be unsettling to realize that you have more giants trying to block your path forward, be encouraged by the power you have through your anointing to walk through every dark valley and to overcome any and all giants. Whether you're dealing with the office gossip thwarting your promotion, supporting a child in recovery, or remaining patient amid chronic pain, you can rest in the comfort of knowing your Good Shepherd is right there with you. He knows your vulnerabilities and will protect you and guard you from every giant. He will provide all you need—even when facing your enemies.

Reflect on the questions below to help remind you of what is true. Giants may come, but their defeat is assured by the power of Christ in you—the Holy Spirit. Then spend some time in prayer as you give thanks and listen closely for the Shepherd's voice. He knows His sheep and His sheep know Him—so take comfort in His presence.

1. What are some of the darkest valleys you have experienced in your life so far? How has walking through these times and places strengthened your faith?

2. Which of the personal, spiritual, and cultural giants described in this chapter resonate the most with you? Which ones are you currently fighting and needing more of the Spirit's power to overcome?

3. Read through Psalm 23 and underline or highlight the images and promises that bring you the most comfort. Based on David's poetic declaration, what do you need to remember as you encounter dark valleys and unexpected giants?

Dear Lord, while David defeated Goliath, endured Saul, and repented from his sins after Bathsheba, I know that You defeated the ultimate giants—condemnation and death. Through Your power that I experience by the gift of Your Spirit within me, I know that I can persevere out of the darkest valley and slay the personal, spiritual, and cultural giants encountered there. Thank You for being my Good Shepherd, willing to lay down Your life for mine. In Jesus' name, Amen.

12

Fear No Evil

Overflowing with Abundance in the Presence of Your Enemies

> God treats you to a feast in the presence of your enemies. Anointed in the Holy Spirit, you will fear no evil—because greater is He who is in you than he who is in the world!

While I'm no celebrity, I do occasionally get recognized in public. Most of the time I don't mind if someone stops to greet me, thank me, or share a prayer request in a restaurant, store, or airport. A few times, however, I've had to set a kind but firm boundary in order to finish my meal, return to my conversation, or make my flight on time. Nearly everyone understands and resumes their reason for being in that location.

Situations with assigned seats take these types of encounters to another level. Most of us have probably been on a plane next to someone who delighted in talking the entire flight despite our attempts to read or sleep. Many of us have also attended a movie, concert, ballgame, or other event and been forced to tolerate nearby neighbors who were less than considerate. As a pastor with a national leadership position, I'm doubly mindful of how I respond in such tricky situations.

If no one knew me or cared who I was, I would still do my best to follow the example of Jesus and respond with kindness and respect, regardless of how inebriated, agitated, or belligerent the person sitting next to me might be acting. I'm also aware that my ministry and leadership role usually attracts greater scrutiny than the average person, which is already stringent enough in our instantly-recorded-and-posted-to-social-media culture. I recall one occasion, however, when the limits of my patience were indeed tested.

Invited to attend an awards banquet, I accepted and looked forward to visiting with some old friends as well as making new acquaintances. When I arrived at my assigned table, I knew a couple of people and introduced myself to the rest of the guests seated with us. The gentleman sitting on my right, I soon learned, knew who I was—and was not a fan. The beginning of the meal began well enough, with all of us making polite conversation and asking perfunctory questions about each other's connections to the event and its hosts.

Shortly after the entrée was served, my right-hand man began asking me questions about our church and ministry. Before I could finish answering, he cut me off and jumped to a variety of political issues before asking specific questions regarding immigration and deportation. I had certainly faced hostile inquiries before, so in this instance I tried to provide a calm, diplomatic response to his challenge. But this man only grew more agitated and came back at me with several "facts" to support his own position.

I made it clear that I have no allegiance to the party of the donkey or the elephant, only the party of the Lamb, Jesus Christ, and then tried to shift to a more benign topic of conversation that would engage our entire table. Unfortunately, my new critic tried to shame me for changing the topic and became even louder and more animated. Guests from nearby tables were now looking over at the commotion caused by the man next to me. One of our hosts came over and whispered in his ear, which finally silenced him. We somehow made it through dessert, but I'm not sure how.

That evening gave new meaning to being at a table in the presence of your enemies!

Come and Join Me

While David never encountered that particular awkward situation, I'm fairly certain he understood my discomfort. We don't know specifically who or which enemies he had in mind when he addressed God in Psalm 23 and said, "You prepare a table before me in the presence of my enemies" (verse 5), but a number of candidates qualify—including Goliath, basically all the Philistines, and King Saul.

If we imagine David at the battlefield, enraged by the disrespectful taunts of the Philistine giant holding the Israelite army hostage with fear, we typically wouldn't include a picnic as part of the situation. But that is, in effect, the situation that David describes in Psalm 23:5. It's as if Goliath is hurling his threats and slurs, eager to take on the audacious youth approaching him without armor, when suddenly David pauses and notices something in the distance between them.

There on the dirty and dusty ground, beautiful blankets, woven rugs, and pillows have been spread and layered. In the middle of this makeshift table, a delicious feast awaits—cheeses, dried meats, olives, fresh figs, and grapes, warm bread, and honey. Jugs of water and wine glisten and offer limitless refreshment. A heavenly voice says, "Come and join Me!" So David calmly sits and begins to eat and drink, clearly grateful and in no hurry to finish anytime soon. Only a short distance away, Goliath can only glare and fume, knowing he is temporarily powerless.

While imaginary, this scene illustrates the essence of what David describes in his prayer found in Psalm 23. God, the loving Shepherd, not only provides everything David needs but goes above and beyond. In addition to leading David into a lush, verdant pasture beside cool, still waters—a rich buffet for any flock of sheep—the Lord provides a rich feast right in the midst of David's enemies. At this surreal banquet, God also anoints David's head with oil and fills his cup until it overflows.

All of these images and descriptions reflect the intentional and thoughtful hospitality that hosts provided to their guests at that time. Hosts not only were responsible for preparing and cooking food but were to make their guests feel welcome, accepted, enjoyed, and cared for. Good hosts would serve the best food available and serve their best wine. They often provided water and towels for guests to wash their dusty feet, often bare or clad in sandals, in order to cleanse and refresh them.

Neglecting or denying hospitality to others was evidence not only of rudeness but of disrespect. You'll recall that the Jewish people did not mingle with Gentiles, whom they considered pagan and unclean. The Samaritan woman at the well mentions this social taboo when Jesus asked her for a drink. In His parable illustrating who we are to regard as our neighbor, Jesus also chooses a Samaritan as the one who shows compassion, care, and hospitality to the man robbed, beaten, and left for dead. Such a breach would likely not have occurred because even if a Samaritan had offered to help, most Jews would have refused their aid.

Extending hospitality with a dinner invitation assumed an offer of kindness, friendship, and connection. People did not invite others into their home unless they were comfortable with such closeness in the bond of breaking bread together. Typically, then as now, you didn't invite enemies into your home for a five-course meal. God, however, is an exceptional host!

A Foothold in Your Fear

David knew that when you're walking through the death-dark valleys of life, giants and enemies will want to attack your vulnerabilities and try to keep you there. Sometimes we're not surprised by their assaults and have already identified them as being against us. Other times, however, we don't realize we're descending into a valley where it's darker until we're blindsided and stumble into a pit. Only then do we realize that we have been betrayed, humiliated, tricked, deceived, lied to, and set up to fail.

You might feel confused and misunderstood and wonder how you could be where you find yourself. You feel stressed by the challenges in all areas of your life, and this latest attack simply pushed you over the edge and knocked you to your knees. You try to get up but weariness overcomes you. Your body aches, your mind blurs, and your heart shudders.

When you're in the bottom of a dark valley, it's hard to see a way out.

You wonder where God is and why He has allowed you to fall into this pit. You not only feel abandoned by the closest people in your life but fear that God may have given up on you as well. You feel responsible for falling into this trap—how could you be so foolish to let this happen?—and then shame sets in, compounding your pain and amplifying your desperation. The story you begin telling yourself is that you have no hope, that it's too late, that you've failed one too many times, that you're done, that there's no way out. Fear tries to consume you as you catastrophize and imagine every calamitous contingency and worst-case scenario.

Then you realize something essential to winning this fight—the identity of your enemy.

With crystal clarity you suddenly see that your battle is not against your boss, your neighbor, your frenemy at work, your disease, your debt, your unemployment, your relationship status, or your addiction. Your battle is not against yourself due to your weaknesses, flaws, and past mistakes. Your fight is not merely against other people, false assumptions, and overwhelming emotions. Your struggle "is not against flesh and blood, but against the rulers, against the authorities, against the powers of this dark world and against the spiritual forces of evil in the heavenly realms" (Ephesians 6:12).

Your battle is against principalities and the powers of darkness.

You're going one-on-one with the devil himself.

The enemy has taken a foothold in your fear.

He has turned into your thoughts and emotions in order to tempt, taunt, and torture you where it hurts most. He wants you to think you're on your own, that everyone else has abandoned you, including God—especially God. But that's simply not true!

What's true is that your Good Shepherd has a sturdy staff to lift you out of the pit.

What's true is that your Good Shepherd is always close by.

What's true is that your Good Shepherd shows you there's nothing to fear.

What's true is that your Good Shepherd not only empowers you to overcome the enemy of your soul but prepares a gourmet meal for you right in front of the devil.

The enemy is not invited and at best can only heckle, mock, and tempt you.

The enemy has no place at your table!

The Way Out Is Up

You've probably been in a restaurant, diner, or fast-food joint and seen a sign declaring, "No shirt, no shoes, no service." Especially during the summertime or in beachside locales, this notice ensures that customers know the bare minimum dress code before they show up and expect to be served. The meal God prepares for you in the presence of the enemy comes with a similar notification: "No fear, no falsehoods, no evil."

When we acknowledge our fear and surrender it to God, we prevent the enemy from gaining a point of entry and elbowing his way onto our table. When we're afraid, we're often willing to seek comfort, safety, and security in whatever seems available in order to alleviate our distress. And the devil knows this, which is why he's quick to offer solutions—money, fame, sex, possessions, ego, basically anything other than God. None of those potential idols help us; indeed, they only make our valley deeper and darker.

The way out is up. When David declares, "Even though I walk through the darkest valley, I will fear no evil," he then proceeds to explain why—"your rod and your staff, they comfort me" (Psalm 23:4). In other words, our divine Shepherd has what it takes to protect us from evil. We see this echoed throughout the Bible, particularly in the New Testament. Several hundred years after David focused our attention on the truth of how God protects and provides for us, Jesus made it even clearer when He taught His disciples how to pray.

> This, then, is how you should pray: "Our Father in heaven, hallowed be your name, your kingdom come, your will be done, on earth as it is in heaven. Give us today our daily bread. And forgive us our debts, as we also have forgiven our debtors. And lead us not into temptation, but deliver us from the evil one."
>
> Matthew 6:9–13

The disciples had never heard anyone pray like Jesus, which prompted them to ask Him to teach them. Rather than the traditional recitation of rabbinical words in the prayers of their Jewish faith, the disciples heard Jesus address God as His Father and speak to Him conversationally, relationally, and intimately. We cannot fully grasp how radical it was to address the almighty and holy God of all creation as "Abba," the familiar, affectionate way young children would address their daddy.

Children, just like sheep, are quite vulnerable.

And every parent knows they would do anything to protect their children.

Above Every Name

God, our loving Abba Father, offers the same protection to us, which is why Jesus invites us to approach God based on our relationship—not on religion. We are not merely God's people, but His beloved sons and daughters. "You have not received a spirit that makes you fearful slaves. Instead, you received God's Spirit when he adopted you as his own children. Now we call him, 'Abba, Father'" (Romans 8:15 NLT).

This shift echoes something of the caring, attuned, protective Shepherd of Psalm 23 and also references how Christ referred to Himself as our Good Shepherd. In fact, Jesus brings the two together, showing the Good Shepherd's relationship with the Father, which in turn reveals how much we are loved by God—so much that the Father sent His Son, Jesus, to be our Shepherd and lay His life down for us, His sheep.

> I am the good shepherd. The good shepherd lays down his life for the sheep. The hired hand is not the shepherd and does not own the sheep. So when he sees the wolf coming, he abandons the sheep and runs away. Then the wolf attacks the flock and scatters it. The man runs away because he is a hired hand and cares nothing for the sheep.
>
> I am the good shepherd; I know my sheep and my sheep know me—just as the Father knows me and I know the Father—and I lay down my life for the sheep.
>
> John 10:11–15

In teaching us how to pray, Jesus also instructs us not only to relate to God as our Abba Father but also to honor His name—"hallowed be your name." While we don't often use "hallow" in our vocabularies today, it carries the full weight of honoring, revering, blessing, and worshiping God's holy name. This is important not only as a declaration of how we love and view God but also as a way of equipping ourselves in battle with the enemy. "GOD's name is a place of protection—good people can run there and be safe" (Proverbs 18:10 MSG).

Calling on God's name provides protection and safety. Calling on the name of Jesus also carries unlimited power and authority.

> Therefore God exalted him to the highest place and gave him the name that is above every name, that at the name of Jesus every knee should bow, in heaven and on earth and under the earth, and every tongue acknowledge that Jesus Christ is Lord, to the glory of God the Father.
>
> Philippians 2:9–11

Jesus informed us, "I will do whatever you ask in my name, so that the Father may be glorified in the Son. You may ask me for anything in my name, and I will do it" (John 14:13–14).

As the early followers of Jesus shared the Good News of the Gospel with everyone they encountered, they made it clear that they were not merely sentimental students or political propagandists of a carpenter from Nazareth, but men and women saved by grace through the death of Christ on the cross and His resurrection through the power of the Holy Spirit, the same Spirit that Jesus had gifted to them at Pentecost. These first believers made it abundantly clear, "Salvation is found in no one else, for there is no other name under heaven given to mankind by which we must be saved" (Acts 4:12). As these believers proceeded to share the Gospel, they made it clear that they had nothing to offer others except for the spiritual power and authority expressed in the name of Jesus. The spiritual power and authority that came with their anointing in the Holy Spirit.

The *same* power and authority you have with your anointing in the Holy Spirit.

When Fear Knocks, Faith Answers

When Jesus instructed us on how to pray, He also said, "And lead us not into temptation, but deliver us from the evil one" (Matthew 6:13). At first glance, this prayer request might seem confusing. In fact, I sometimes have people point to this verse and ask, "Doesn't this mean that God leads us into temptation? Why would He do that?"

And my short answer is always, "No, God does not lead us into temptation." And then I explain that perhaps a more accurate, precise translation of the original Greek reads, "Do not allow us *to be led* into temptation." In other words, remind us of the power we have to overcome the temptations we're going to face.

Notice the vast difference here. It's assumed that we will be tempted by the enemy, so we seek God's help to resist and remain strong in our faith. God never leads us to sin—we seem to get there just fine without any help! Instead, God strengthens us and empowers us to resist the snares the devil loves to spring on us, which he does constantly. He is always prowling, planning, and plotting to bring us down. "Be alert and of sober mind. Your enemy the devil prowls around like a roaring lion looking for someone to devour" (1 Peter 5:8).

If you're not alert, then it's easy to stay stuck in the pit of the valley.

If you're not sober-minded, then it's easy to become the devil's punching bag.

If you're not focused on God, then it's easy to be distracted by giants.

But you have spiritual armor and the power to overcome!

Spiritual warfare is not militarizing your faith; it is simply utilizing the spiritual defenses you've been given to overcome the darkness.

Spiritual warfare requires confronting the enemy, calling out his lies, and anchoring yourself to God's truth.

Spiritual warfare means you proactively bind the devil and his schemes against you, against your family, and against your anointing in the name of Jesus.

Spiritual warfare means that when fear knocks on your door, you answer with faith!

More Than Enough

When you live in the fullness of your anointing, fear has no power over you. Yes, you will walk through some dark valleys. Yes, the enemy will try to prop up giants to get in your way. But you will always come out the other side with those giants at your feet! "You, dear children, are from God and have overcome them, because the one who is in you is greater than the one who is in the world" (1 John 4:4).

You, my friend, should not be afraid—you are an overcomer.

You are anointed to prove hell wrong.

You are trampling on everything hell places in your path.

Without a doubt, every single day you will confront a constant bombardment of negativity, toxic atmospheres, adversity, conflicts, delusional dynamics, false ideologies, social constructs, principalities, and powers of darkness all with one objective—to convince you that you don't have what it takes! Like Goliath across the battlefield, they will yell, post, comment, and troll you with their taunts:

"You will never defeat the giants in your generation!"

"You will never occupy God's promises."

"You will never conquer new territories for Him."

"You will never overcome us—no way!"

Let me exclaim once more, you are anointed to prove hell wrong!

When you have faith in the finished work of Christ, you have no fear.

When you step into every chapter and season of life with the certainty of 2 Corinthians 5:7, that you walk by faith and not by sight, you feast while the enemy fumes.

When you live with the sacred algorithm of Romans 10:17 that faith comes from hearing the Good News about Christ, you rest in the power of truth.

When you stand empowered with the promise of Matthew 21:22, that you can pray for anything, and if you have faith, you will receive it, then you can move mountains!

When you walk and talk, live, give, and forgive with that kind of faith, with the faith *in* Christ, and the faith *of* Christ, and faith *through* Christ's Spirit in you, then you know you have more than enough of what it takes!

Then you can stand up as David did through his actions.

Then you can rise up as David did through his accomplishments.

Then you can speak up as David did through his psalms and his writings.

Because you are crucified with Christ and now it is Christ living in you (see Galatians 2:20).

Because you abide in His Word and His Word abides in you (see John 15:7)

Because you are a new creation with Christ as your everything (see 2 Corinthians 5:17; Colossians 3:11).

Because of the five stones of faith you've been given—identity, intimacy, integrity, influence, innovation—you will feast in the presence of your enemies.

You will fear no evil because you are anointed by God's Spirit!

Selecting Your Stone

Fear no longer has power over you when you live in the fullness of your anointing in God's Spirit. Use the questions below to help you absorb the reality of this truth in your life and in your pursuit of fulfilling your divine purpose. Take a few minutes and allow this time of reflection and prayer to serve as an opportunity for spiritual rest beside still waters and spiritual nourishment from the table spread before you in the presence of your enemies. Remember that you have been anointed and chosen by God—He fills your cup and it's overflowing.

1. Generally speaking, do you consider yourself a fearful person? What are some of your greatest fears, and how have you usually responded when faced with them?

2. How have you seen your faith overcome fear as you continue to grow in the fullness of your anointing in God's Spirit? How has God equipped you to stare down giants and to march through dark valleys as you surrender your fear to Him?

3. What does it mean for you to share a feast prepared by God in the presence of your enemies? How does this image and metaphor comfort and reassure you that you can face anything the enemy may throw your way?

Dear Abba Father, dear Good Shepherd, dear Spirit of God, I am so grateful that fear has no power to undermine my faith and to hold me captive in the dark valleys. Remind me of the power I have in You to surrender my fear and to overcome the enemy and any giants in my way. Thank You for loving me and guarding my steps through dark valleys and leading me into the glorious light of Your mercy and truth. Shine through me, Lord, so that others may also give You glory and be drawn to You, rescued by You, and redeemed by You. In Jesus' name, Amen.

FIFTH STONE

INNOVATION

Anointed to Slay Your Giants with More

> Do not conform to the pattern of this world, but be transformed by the renewing of your mind. Then you will be able to test and approve what God's will is—his good, pleasing and perfect will.
>
> Romans 12:2

13

Anointed for Every New Season

Occupying All of God's Promises

> To everything there is a season under heaven, but God's promises remain the same. When you live in power of the Holy Spirit, you're anointed for every age and stage of life.

Fall was my favorite season when I was growing up.

In the Lehigh Valley of Pennsylvania, where I spent most of my childhood, I relied on the trees not only as a seasonal barometer but also as an indicator of how far along we were in any given season. Usually in September each year, I would notice the rich green canopy of summer leaves turn lighter and brighter until one day they miraculously changed colors. Instead of the emerald palette of summer greens, autumn announced itself in gradient shades of yellow and amber, russet and tan, pale orange and bright scarlet.

I loved fall because school resumed, and I not only enjoyed seeing my friends again but anticipated the challenges of new courses and the knowledge they yielded. Yes, I was the geeky kid who actually did the assigned reading and enjoyed the homework—which I learned quickly to keep to myself. There were pep rallies and football games, harvest dances and bonfires, hayrides and pumpkin patches. Cool air turned chilly until the first big frost, and then it was usually cold enough for winter coats.

When I moved to California as an adult, I not only missed the kind of falls I had grown up enjoying but missed the pronounced distinction of all four seasons. Central and Northern California, where my wife and I settled, arguably has four seasons, although it's often hard to tell where one ends and the next begins. Some locals informed us that they basically had two seasons—hot and dry in summer and cool and wet in winter. While spring and fall still make appearances, they seem to last only two or three weeks before ushering in the next.

Seasons of life can sometimes be just as unpredictable. It's true some seasons have clear beginning and end points, such as parenting. We knew from the time we started having kids that our lives would be forever changed along with our lifestyle rhythms. Once they were grown and moved out on their own, we transitioned into a season of being empty nesters. A few years later, we became grandparents, which started yet another new season.

Relationships often go through seasonal cycles as well. Whether with family, friends, or coworkers, people's needs may change as they endure various life experiences together. Our church and ministry have certainly gone through various seasons as well, whether adjusting to new growth, the need for larger facilities, or expansion into other locations. Regardless of the kinds of seasons you encounter, they all include adapting to change—which can sometimes be scary, uncomfortable, and disorienting.

As anointed followers of Jesus, however, we need not fear any of these changes. Because we have the certainty of something that never shifts—God's presence, power, and purpose in our lives through His Spirit within us.

Troops and Treasure

While we are anointed for every new season we encounter, we sometimes get in the way of how God is at work in our lives. This may result from growing impatient with God's timing, manipulating people and circumstances to suit our desires, and taking matters into our own hands. Sometimes even when we've reached the maturation of our anointing, we can still succumb to our human pride and self-reliance. Regardless of the season and circumstances of our lives, living in the fullness of our anointing requires us to remain attuned to God's Spirit and to follow His guidance.

Even toward the end of his life, David still struggled with his tendency to take matters into his own hands. While he restored his relationship with God after sinning with Bathsheba, this messy situation was not the only incident in which David sinned against God. Toward the end of his life and reign, David conducted a census of Israel that resulted in severe consequences for the nation of Israel. Following victorious battles with the Philistines, David ordered Joab, the captain of his army, to go throughout all twelve tribes and count the people. Typically, a census was conducted in order to enlist men in the king's armies and to collect taxes—the two primary ways monarchs maintained their power base, troops, and treasure.

David's motivation for this decision is unclear, but his choice illustrates the way that sometimes God permits us to be tempted in order to strengthen our reliance on Him instead of ourselves.

> Once again God's anger blazed out against Israel. He tested David by telling him, "Go and take a census of Israel and Judah." So David gave orders to Joab and the army officers under him, "Canvass all the tribes of Israel, from Dan to Beersheba, and get a count of the population. I want to know the number."
>
> But Joab resisted the king: "May your God multiply people by the hundreds right before the eyes of my master the king, but why on earth would you do a thing like this?"
>
> Nevertheless, the king insisted, and so Joab and the army officers left the king to take a census of Israel. . . . They canvassed the whole country and after nine months and twenty days arrived back in Jerusalem. Joab gave the results of the census to the king: 800,000 able-bodied fighting men in Israel; in Judah 500,000.
>
> But when it was all done, David was overwhelmed with guilt because he had counted the people, replacing trust with statistics. And David

> prayed to God, "I have sinned badly in what I have just done. But now God forgive my guilt—I've been really stupid."
>
> 2 Samuel 24:1–10 MSG

Notice that Joab immediately questioned David's decision by boldly asking, "Why on earth would you do such a thing?" His inquiry and reluctance reveal that this was not a good idea and that Joab thought David should know better. But David's royal decree trumped Joab's common sense, and only in hindsight could the king realize something we've all thought at one time or another: *I've been really stupid.*

Come-to-Your-Senses Seasons

After all his years of relying on his anointing, after relying on God throughout his decades-long reign, it suddenly seemed as if David wanted to increase his power base by counting heads. As he quickly realized after the results came in, David had replaced his trust in God's sovereignty and provision with data and statistics. David apparently saw his mistake right away and probably wondered, "What was I thinking?"

After giving in to temptation, you may have had a similar awakening. Like the prodigal son in Jesus' parable, we come to our senses and realize that we're feeding pigs and envying their food rather than returning to our loving Father (see Luke 15:16–17). Like Paul writing to the early Church in Rome, we wonder, "Why do I do what I don't want to do? I don't understand myself" (see Romans 7:15). While our failures may appear reckless or impulsive, we usually see in hindsight we allowed ourselves to slip back into our previous default mindset of self-reliance.

In this season of his life, David was likely considering the legacy he would leave behind. He was looking ahead at who would become king after him (more about this momentarily) and the economic and military health of Israel as a nation. I suspect he wanted not only to handpick his successor to the throne but to ensure that he left Israel in the best shape possible—perhaps especially since David knew God was angry at the way the Israelites tended to disobey repeatedly despite the many victories and blessings He bestowed on them. It all seems logical enough, which is exactly what the enemy hopes will appeal to us. This perspective is confirmed by another account of this incident. "Satan rose up against Israel and incited David to take a census of Israel" (1 Chronicles 21:1).

When you're living in the fulfillment of your anointing, you will still face temptations—but not necessarily the same ones you faced on your way to where you are. Instead, the enemy will tailor temptations to appeal to all the circumstances of your present season. He knows your weaknesses and insecurities and how to appeal to your ego in a way that seems to make sense in the moment.

I remember someone from another ministry once coming to me to confess that they had embezzled funds that they intended to replace before anyone realized they were missing. Their explanation was that they knew for certain that God had brought them into leadership in this ministry and would want them to remain in charge. But the only way to stay there, as they saw it at the time, was if they had more compensation.

Can you recall a time when you yielded to temptation only to realize your disobedience and lack of trust in God? A time when you came to your senses and wondered how you could have been so blind to the enemy's snare?

While I've never been tempted to embezzle funds or take a census of those entrusted to my care, I know that I'm not above being tempted and tested. No one is. Which is why we must remain humble and reliant on the power and wisdom of the Spirit within us and not our own understanding and limited human perspective.

The Lord gave David a choice of three consequences, and David selected the option that allowed him to appeal to the Lord's mercy. Nonetheless, a plague claimed at least seventy thousand lives throughout Israel before God intervened and ended the epidemic (see 2 Samuel 24:15; 1 Chronicles 21:14). David's failure to rely on the power of God resulted in a ripple effect that devastated many lives. It's sobering to realize that our sin can affect so many other people adversely, but that's all the more reason to remain anchored by faith to the truth of God's Word.

Anointed for Legacy

If my speculation on David's motive for conducting a census—that he was taking control of his legacy—is partly accurate, it's striking to see how his successor ascends to the throne. We're told that David grew old and as "the years caught up with him," he had a clear sense that his life was drawing to a close (see 1 Kings 1). He apparently suffered from chills and couldn't get warm regardless of how many blankets covered him. Even having a beautiful young woman as his caretaker didn't seem to comfort the ailing king.

In this winter season of life, David once again faced some family drama. Apparently, everyone, particularly David's son Adonijah, could tell that the king's death was imminent, which would create a power vacuum in the nation of Israel. We're told that this would-be royal heir was not only spoiled by David while growing up but also quite handsome. No surprise then that Adonijah had the swagger to proclaim himself as the next king before his father had even died (see 1 Kings 1:5–6)!

Acting on his intentions, Adonijah organized a big inaugural event, including animal sacrifices, local dignitaries, and VIPs—except for his father, of course—as well as Nathan the prophet, his half-brother Solomon, and Solomon's bodyguards. They were intended to find out after the fact. Only Nathan knew, and he had informed Bathsheba, now David's wife and the mother of several children, including Solomon. She had already asked David to promise her that Solomon would take his place on the throne, which the king agreed to fulfill. With Adonijah's self-proclaimed coronation imminent, Bathsheba thought it the perfect time to verify her husband's promise.

David not only vowed before God to uphold his promise to Bathsheba concerning their son's future but took immediate action. He gathered a small band of confidants and instructed them to proceed with anointing Solomon as ruler over Israel and Judah, which they did (see 1 Kings 1:32–40). When Adonijah's pre-coronation dinner party heard the commotion and learned the reason, they were terrified that Solomon and David would punish their presumption and insurrection. But after Adonijah bowed before the newly crowned King Solomon, his half-brother spared his life and sent him home.

David upheld his vow to God and his promise to Bathsheba, and the shepherd king of Israel secured the legacy of his anointing.

A Season for Every Purpose

Solomon would go on to rule Israel for forty years just as his father David had reigned for four decades. Known for his wisdom, wealth, and writings, Solomon would fulfill his father's dream and undertake the building of the temple in Jerusalem. Its completion took approximately seven years and featured elaborate details of gold, ivory, and other precious resources. For all his success, though, Solomon endured seasons and valleys similar to some that his father had faced. Most historians and scholars believe Solomon wrote Ecclesiastes in the midst of struggling with his successes.

While some passages of Ecclesiastes can be challenging for contemporary readers, the narrator makes his purpose clear—to leave a legacy of wisdom based on all he has seen, learned, observed, and experienced. "I was a wise teacher with much understanding, and I collected a number of proverbs that I had carefully studied. Then I tried to explain these things in the best and most accurate way" (Ecclesiastes 12:9–10 CEV). His intentions manifest themselves through the many proverbs and axioms of truth inserted within the narrative passages.

One of the most profound lessons the teacher in Ecclesiastes shares is also one of the most challenging—a struggle that remains both timeless and urgent for us today. He reveals the consequences of getting everything you ever wanted and discovering it doesn't satisfy your soul. The narrator describes his vast riches, many wives, and reputation as the wisest, most famous person in Jerusalem—and yet he finds all his accomplishments ultimately unfulfilling (see Ecclesiastes 2:1–11). "With all my wisdom I tried to understand everything that happens here on earth. And God has made this so hard for us humans to do. I have seen it all, and everything is just as senseless as chasing the wind" (Ecclesiastes 1:13–14 CEV).

Nonetheless, Solomon's observations offer astute wisdom and insight on life and its many seasons. One poetic passage in particular describes a truth that may seem obvious to us but remains worthy of contemplation:

> Everything on earth
> has its own time
>   and its own season.
> There is a time
> for birth and death,
>   planting and reaping,
> for killing and healing,
>   destroying and building,
> for crying and laughing,
>   weeping and dancing,
> for throwing stones
> and gathering stones,
>   embracing and parting.
> There is a time
> for finding and losing,
>   keeping and giving,
> for tearing and sewing,
>   listening and speaking.
> There is also a time
> for love and hate,
>   for war and peace.
>
> Ecclesiastes 3:1–8 CEV

Heeding the wisdom of Solomon's observations, we realize that even when we don't like our circumstances and season of life, we can trust that God remains with us. While events, relationships, weather patterns, finances, family responsibilities, lifestyles, technology, AI capabilities, grocery prices, music trends, and fashion styles may continually fluctuate, we have bedrock truth as our foundation. We live in the certainty that "Jesus Christ is the same yesterday and today and forever" (Hebrews 13:8).

We know that even in our most painful, frustrating, and unproductive seasons, God continues to bless us and sustain us. "Every good and perfect gift is from above, coming down from the Father of the heavenly lights, who does not change like shifting shadows" (James 1:17). And perhaps the most perfect gift of all is the Holy Spirit within us. "And I will ask the Father, and he will give you another advocate to help you and be with you forever" (John 14:16). We never have to fear change because we serve the only One whose love, power, mercy, and goodness remain constant.

No matter the season, our faith remains solid.

All-Season Anointing

God anointed David for every new season of his life. From a human perspective, David was the unlikeliest of candidates, yet God saw beyond appearances and knew David's heart—a heart after God's own heart. Consequently, David was anointed not once or twice but three times (see 1 Samuel 16:13; 2 Samuel 2:4; 5:3). Each anointing marked a major milestone in the life of this shepherd from Bethlehem who became king in the city that still bears his name, the City of David.

You'll recall that David's first anointing was in private. "So as David stood there among his brothers, Samuel took the flask of olive oil he had brought and anointed David with the oil. And the Spirit of the LORD came powerfully upon David from that day on" (1 Samuel 16:13 NLT).

David received his first anointing in the presence of his family members.

David received his first anointing and served King Saul and his brothers.

David received his first anointing and then waited until God said, "Now is the time!"

When we are first anointed with the gift of God's Spirit, our spiritual development often follows a trajectory similar to David's. When God first chooses you and you accept Him into your heart, He anoints the private you before He anoints the public you.

He anoints you to serve before He anoints you to lead.

He anoints you in the presence of your family before He anoints you in the presence of your enemies.

He anoints you to wait before He anoints you to win!

With David's first anointing, this farm boy who wasn't even old enough to be in the king's army dared to go against a giant terrifying everyone else on the battlefront. Through the power of the Spirit that came powerfully on David at his first anointing, he defeated the giant coming after his family and after his generation. He didn't listen to the doubters, discouragers, and deluded who couldn't imagine David winning—especially after refusing Saul's armor!

Just like David, and even more because of Jesus, you are anointed to bring down the giants in your family and in your generation.

You are not anointed to take selfies.

You are not anointed to scroll headlines and post comments.

You are not anointed to express your opinions or fill the world with your feelings.

You are anointed to persevere through dark valleys without fear and to slay the giants who stand in your way.

You are anointed to grow strong in your faith, to resist temptation, and to repent and return to the Lord your God when you stumble.

You are anointed to do what no one else but you can do.

Why? Because the Holy Spirit lives inside you!

David received his second anointing after waiting for God to prepare and equip him for more. He received partial fulfillment of his calling by being anointed king over Judah. David was ready for more, and God anointed him a second time and entrusted him with royal responsibilities and resources. David needed more experience before ruling the entire kingdom, so he began by leading the tribe of Judah.

If you haven't experienced your second anointing already, then you need to know that it's coming. You need to remember that God has been using every circumstance, conversation, conflict, and collaboration to season you for more responsibilities and resources. When you're faithful in the small things, He entrusts you with bigger things.

David's third anointing occurred about seven and a half years after he was anointed king over Judah. Saul had died and the twelve tribes were in turmoil from political posturing within and persistent Philistine attacks without. They needed a leader who could unite them as one nation under God, and David was finally ready to receive the fulfillment of his anointing.

Whether you're aware of receiving your third anointing or not, God is preparing you to fulfill and complete the divine purpose for which He created you. All that you've experienced and endured has been for a time such as this. Relying on the Holy Spirit, David's power increased from season to season and strength to strength. Yours will continue to flourish as well.

No matter what season you're in, you are anointed for more.

If your season is winter, then spring is on its way.

If your season is summer, then fall's harvest will be abundant.

If your season is raising children, then prepare them for adulthood.

If your season is treading water, then get ready to walk on solid ground.

If your season is illness, then get ready to be well.

If your season is debt, then get ready to receive God's blessings.

If your season is grief, then get ready to laugh.

If your season is loss, then get ready to gain.

If your season is anxiety, then get ready for peace.

If your season is depression, then get ready for joy.

Sun, rain, wind, and snow—you have an all-season anointing!

No matter what your season, your anointing guarantees God's presence, power, protection, and provision in your life!

Selecting Your Stone

Amid the daily demands you face, you might have lost your perspective on the season you're in. Even when you know it's a season of waiting, of growing, of developing, of maturing, the losses of life and assaults from the enemy can hinder your vision. Using the questions below, ask the Holy Spirit with you to open the eyes of your heart and refresh your vision. Seek clarity about your current season and how God wants you to steward your time, energy, talents, and resources. Then spend some time in prayer, thanking God for the many gifts of your all-season anointing.

1. How would you describe or delineate the major seasons of your life so far? What challenges and blessings are you now experiencing in your current season?

2. When have you returned to relying on your own power or tried to take control of a situation or relationship rather than trust God and wait on His timing? What did you learn from that incident?

3. As you look ahead and consider your remaining time in this life, what do you want your spiritual legacy to be? How has your anointing already benefited others around you?

Dear God, whether my seasons seem to change slowly or rapidly, whether my circumstances are predictably calm or unexpectedly choppy, I am grateful for the constancy of Your love. The more seasons I experience in this life, the more I realize that I cannot overcome the valleys and giants of life without relying on Your power. Help me not to get ahead of You and slide back into default ways of trying to take control or accelerate beyond my human capacity. Remind me that I can rest in Your Spirit regardless of my life's season and the spiritual weather it may bring, trusting You for everything I need. In Jesus' name, Amen.

14

Five-Stone Foundation

Building with the Tools of Your Anointing

> Identity, intimacy, integrity, influence, and innovation create a solid foundation for building your faith on rock, not sand. Using these five stones as building blocks, you inhabit the fulfillment of your anointing!

If you've ever visited a construction site, then you know it can be chaos.

Recently I visited a friend who was building a new workplace for his family-owned business. They had outgrown their small facility where his grandfather had first launched and found a suitable property that was reasonably priced for the area. While he hired a contractor to serve as project manager, he and his team were also hoping to do as much of the work as possible to save on costs.

On the day I showed up to visit, at least a half dozen workers were getting started. Most of the exterior had been completed—foundation, floors, walls, and roof. The interior, however, still required a great deal of work before it would be functionable for business. As we dodged drywall, two-by-fours, and sawhorses, my friend apologized for the mess. I assured him no apologies were necessary because chaos is almost always part of the process for creating order and beauty.

My friend then shared that the secret to constructing through the chaos of the building process was having the right tools. He held up a few examples, including a power drill, wood lathe, nail gun, and electrical pliers and explained that most tools have become more sophisticated and precise thanks to technology. I professed my appreciation and complimented him on how his vision was coming to life from the ground up.

Driving away, I lingered on our conversation and all the various tools required to construct and complete a house, store, or building. And, as it often does, my mind saw parallels between my friend's building site and the Christian faith.

Both require persevering through chaos in order to create the vision.

Both require using the right tools at the right time for the right job.

Both require collaborative commitment and joint effort to produce results.

There's also one significant difference: Our earthly structures will not last. You've likely seen old buildings, hastily built homes, and strip malls demolished in order to build new structures. Even buildings that have endured for decades or centuries can burn or be obliterated by tornadoes and hurricanes. No human-made structure will last.

The spiritual house we build, however, lasts for eternity.

Solid as a Rock

Without a doubt, spiritual construction relies on our anointing. As we've seen throughout the previous chapters, relying on the power of the Holy Spirit within us allows us to pursue and fulfill our God-given purpose just as David did. Through each stage and season of our lives, our anointing in the Spirit empowers us to stand strong in our faith, grow closer to God, and become more like Jesus. As we mature, we become more adept at using the spiritual resources available to us. We remove the armor that others impose on us, just as David refused Saul's armor, and we trust that God has prepared and equipped us for anything we face.

One of the essential reasons we can persevere through the inevitable storms of life comes from our foundation. In one of his instructive parables, Jesus explained the vital importance of what a house is built upon.

> Therefore everyone who hears these words of mine and puts them into practice is like a wise man who built his house on the rock. The rain came down, the streams rose, and the winds blew and beat against that house; yet it did not fall, because it had its foundation on the rock. But everyone who hears these words of mine and does not put them into practice is like a foolish man who built his house on sand. The rain came down, the streams rose, and the winds blew and beat against that house, and it fell with a great crash.
>
> Matthew 7:24–27

While most people might say they want to build their house on the security of rock-solid faith, they may not be willing to pay the cost—putting into practice the teachings of Jesus. If they don't pay the cost, those decisions leave them on a shaky foundation built on sand, easily moved by the cultural currents and ideological winds around them. In order to build our spiritual house on the rock, we must put our faith into action, aligning what we believe with how we live our lives.

Our relationship with God is not built on merit but on grace. No one is worthy, yet God desires for all to be saved through the sacrifice His Son made on the cross. Salvation by grace is not based on what we do or don't do, as the basis of God's grace is His love for us. When we experience His love, accept salvation by grace, and receive the gift of the Holy Spirit, we naturally change from the inside out.

Once we're anointed in the Spirit, our actions, attitudes, and behaviors align with our beliefs, convictions, and the truth of God's Word. James asks, "What good is it, my brothers and sisters, if someone claims to have faith but has no deeds? Can such faith save them?" (James 2:14). After explaining why and how faith and deeds synchronize when we have God's Spirit in us, James concludes, "As the body without the spirit is dead, so faith without deeds is dead" (James 2:26). Our anointing aligns our behavior with our beliefs. Empowered by the Holy Spirit, we grow in our faith and desire to love and serve others.

Simply put, once the Holy Spirit dwells in us, we supernaturally produce spiritual fruit!

Prepared Prophetically on Purpose

The Holy Spirit within us transforms our hearts and empowers us through our anointing to fulfill our God-given purpose. This is the construction process we see throughout the life of David. And as you're well aware by now, I believe the five stones he selected prior to his showdown with Goliath symbolically resonate with urgent significance for us today. David had to clear away the contempt, condescension, disdain, and doubts of those around him. He had to try on Saul's armor, but he found it a hindrance rather than a help in his battle.

Instead, David relied on how God had already prepared him for this fight. "Then he took his staff in his hand, chose five smooth stones from the stream, put them in the pouch of his shepherd's bag and, with his sling in his hand, approached the Philistine" (1 Samuel 17:40). These five smooth stones not only became the weapons for David's slingshot but also metaphorically provided the foundation for the life he would build through the power of God's Spirit.

Faced with the disrespect and disdain of a giant warrior, David chose five smooth stones—strategically, prophetically, and with purpose. While it only took one stone planted in the center of Goliath's forehead to topple him to the ground, David chose five because he wanted to be prepared. And even after defeating Goliath, David knew there might be more giants waiting to attack.

Today, God has given us five stones to defeat the Goliaths standing in the way of our God-ordained destiny. But these five stones also serve as a foundation for our anointing while providing the spiritual tools and resources needed to build the life God has designed us to live. Through the power of our anointing in God's Spirit, we have five stones that we can use to slay giants: identity, intimacy, integrity, influence, and innovation.

But these five stones are also building blocks for our spiritual growth, development, and maturation. Each one functions in unique ways to support our growth and the life of faith we build upon it through our beliefs and actions. While each of the five has thematically shaped the message of previous chapters, it's helpful to examine them individually once more and see how they overlap and interconnect. When you see the comprehensive scope of their support, you realize their capacity to support your growth throughout your entire life. Let's consider each one within the context of this foundational support.

Stone 1: Identity—You are everything Jesus paid for on the cross

Identity is not what culture says about you.
Identity is not even what you say about you.
Identity is what God says about you.

Your primary descriptor is not black, white, brown, Hispanic, or charismatic. Your number one descriptor is this: You are a born-again child of God. A beloved son or daughter of the living King. You are everything Jesus paid for on the cross. "I have been crucified with Christ and I no longer live, but Christ lives in me. The life I now live in the body, I live by faith in the Son of God, who loved me and gave himself for me" (Galatians 2:20).

When you know who you are, you refuse to be anyone else. You refuse to conform to cultural expectations, be enslaved by your past, or be defined by your failures.

Your identity is anchored in the fullness of the finished work of Christ—and when you walk in that finished fullness, every giant of doubt and deception falls. "For we are God's masterpiece. He has created us anew in Christ Jesus, so we can do the good things he planned for us long ago" (Ephesians 2:10 NLT).

You become what you pray, how you love, and why you serve. God's Spirit lives in you. Your body is a sacred temple of His presence dwelling in you. You are co-heirs with Jesus, saved by grace, and anointed in the Holy Spirit.

Stone 2: Intimacy—You have left the shallow for the deep

Spiritual intimacy is the weapon that deepens our faith and gives us divine authority. Your supernatural relationship with God is sealed by the Holy Spirit within you. "But whoever is united with the Lord is one with him in spirit" (1 Corinthians 6:17).

You cannot defeat your Goliath while standing in the shallow waters of superficial faith and cultural Christianity. You must leave behind *transactional religion* and step into *transformational relationship*. Intimacy with God is the stepping stone for your jump from the old ways to the new.

Spiritual intimacy transforms how you pray. You no longer pray for God to bless you; you pray for God to make you a blessing. You no longer pray for God to simply answer your prayers; you pray that God makes you the answer to someone else's prayer. You no longer pray only for your own needs; you pray for the needs of others.

Intimacy with Christ is about the reconciliation of the vertical and horizontal planes of the cross—what I call the Lamb's agenda. This intersection encompasses sanctification and service, conviction and compassion, covenant and community, truth and love. This kind of spiritual intimacy reflects the divine love of John 3:16 and the faith-fueled actions illustrated in Matthew 25.

Intimacy is the platform that sustains public influence.

When you walk in spiritual intimacy, you cannot be shaken.

Stone 3: Integrity—You are anointed to live whole and holy

Integrity means wholeness—radical wholeness that comes from the healing touch of God. Radical wholeness that takes the jagged pieces of your life and produces God's masterpiece. When you live in the fullness of your anointing, spiritual integrity solidifies your faith. "May God himself, the God of peace, sanctify you through and through. May your whole spirit, soul and body be kept blameless at the coming of our Lord Jesus Christ. The one who calls you is faithful, and he will do it" (1 Thessalonians 5:23–24).

When you are whole, you are *unstoppable*. The wholeness of integrity does not mean you have never been broken. It means your wholeness has been restored by God, stronger than before.

When your integrity is greater than your influence, nothing can stop you.

When you are driven by anointing rather than ambition, nothing can stop you.

When your hunger for righteousness is greater than your fear of criticism, nothing can stop you.

When your praise is louder than your pain, nothing can stop you.

When your character outlasts your charisma, nothing can stop you.

When you choose purpose over popularity, nothing can stop you.

Integrity is about holiness. Integrity is not just about avoiding sin but about being so whole, so aligned with God's truth, that the world cannot shake you. "Be holy, because I am holy" (1 Peter 1:16). You remain grounded no matter how many other forces try to shake, rattle, and roll you. You stand your ground before giants and march through dark valleys into God's light.

Stone 4: Influence—You are called to lead

David's victory over Goliath gave him influence, and God calls us to shift culture, not be shaped by it. We are called to reflect God's glory, love unconditionally, and serve supernaturally. We focus on worship and waiting on God rather than winning.

The altar precedes the platform.

Influence is about more than platforms or popularity. It is about standing for truth when others sit in silence. Spiritual influence is about leading with conviction rather than convenience. It is about using your gifts and resources to expand the Kingdom of God and not the kingdom of self. "You are the light of the world. A town built on a hill cannot be hidden" (Matthew 5:14).

If you are filled with the Holy Spirit, you cannot remain in the shadows. Your business, leadership, and platform must serve the Kingdom. Your motivation becomes fixed on eternal significance, not on earthly treasures.

Influence is not about a microphone; it's about a message.

Influence is not about fame; it's about faithfulness.

Influence is not about being liked; it's about being light.

When you pick up the stone of influence, you stake a territorial claim for the Kingdom.

When your integrity is greater than your influence, nothing can stop you.

When you are driven by anointing rather than ambition, nothing can stop you.

When your hunger for righteousness is greater than your fear of criticism, nothing can stop you.

When your praise is louder than your pain, nothing can stop you.

When your character outlasts your charisma, nothing can stop you.

When you choose purpose over popularity, nothing can stop you.

Integrity is not just about avoiding sin. It is about being so whole, so aligned with God's truth that the world cannot shake you. Your integrity sets an example that allows those who follow after you to become greater than yourself. Humility is the wineskin that sustains God's favor. Living in the power of your anointing, your cup of integrity overflows.

Stone 5: Innovation—God is doing a new thing in you and through you

The final stone is innovation, which means ingenuity, creativity, and new ideas.

David didn't defeat Goliath with Saul's armor; he innovated by using what God had equipped him with. He didn't have sword and shield, but he had a staff and slingshot. He noticed what was within reach and selected five smooth stones.

The early Church innovated, spreading the Gospel in new and powerful ways.

God is still calling His people to create, build, and pioneer. "See, I am doing a new thing! Now it springs up; do you not perceive it? I am making a way in the wilderness and streams in the wasteland" (Isaiah 43:19). Created in the image of God and anointed by His Spirit, we are called to bring new perspectives to old conflicts. We're called to rely on resilience and resourcefulness instead of natural resources and artificial intelligence.

Innovation in the Kingdom means stepping out of comfort zones where we're used to playing it safe and into danger zones where we're required to risk. Innovation means we refuse to be locked in old mindsets when God is birthing something new. We embrace change, knowing that God is always ahead of us. We become problem-solvers, not just problem-identifiers.

The world doesn't need a Church that imitates—it needs a Church that innovates. Measured not by reach but by righteousness, innovation multiplies influence. Innovation creates from the abundance of our anointing. Innovation creates from the wellspring of our anointed imagination.

Ignited by the Spirit's inspiration, we discover innovation!

You're Still Standing

David didn't just pick up the stones—he used them. Through the power of your anointing, you have access to what each of these stones symbolizes. But having access isn't the same as using them as the building blocks of a rock-solid faith. It's time to take up your five stones and ask yourself what you will do with them.

Will you embrace your identity in Christ?

Will you cultivate deep spiritual intimacy?

Will you walk in unwavering integrity?

Will you step boldly into influence?

Will you pioneer with innovation?

Jesus said that anyone who hears His words and puts them into practice is like a wise builder who constructs his house on rock. Conversely, anyone who hears Jesus' teachings and does not put them into practice is like a foolish builder who constructs his house on sand. When the rains come, the streams rise, and the winds blow, one house will still be standing, and one will collapse with a great crash (see Matthew 7:24–27). When you build your house on a five-stone foundation, your faith will endure even the harshest storms of life.

David built his faith on the rock, and his house is still standing today. At an early age, he faced adversity and had to rely on God to empower him. As a shepherd tending his family's flocks, David fought the bear and he fought the lion—and defeated them both. Even in the midst of danger, David was still standing.

David faced a giant Philistine bully named Goliath who had terrorized the king and his entire army for forty days. David could not allow this enemy to disrespect the God of Israel, so he accepted that he must confront a warrior despite the great disparity in their size, experience, and equipment. David chose his five smooth stones and charged toward the danger when everyone else ran away. Logically, rationally, and historically, David didn't seem to have a chance—but he was the one still standing.

Throughout his life, David kept standing because the foundation of his faith could not be shaken. The storms came in the form of Saul's madness and jealousy, battles with the Philistines, and David's own sinful spiral into adultery and murder. Despite the hardships, despite the odds, and despite the external adversaries and internal insecurities, David was still standing.

You, too, are still standing.

Your house is built with a five-stone foundation and will not be shaken.

You've endured storms, giants, valleys, and so much more, and you're still standing.

The enemy has attacked you with the expectation of defeating you, but you're still standing.

You fought depression and you fought anxiety, but you're still standing.

You fought trauma and you fought drama, but you're still standing.

You fought betrayal and you fought brokenness, but you're still standing.

You fought external enemies and internal enemies, and you're still standing.

You had to fight some thoughts off. You had to fight some temptations off. You had to fight some hell off. But you're still standing.

Why are you still standing?

Because *greater is He that is in you than he that is in the world* (see 1 John 4:4).

Because the Word of God never fails (see Luke 1:37).

Because everything that you fought was already defeated by Jesus on the cross.

Everything you have confronted has already been defeated.

Everything you're fighting was confronted and conquered on the cross two thousand years ago!

You're not supposed to still be standing. After being storm tossed, knocked down, battered and bruised, dismissed and discounted, overwhelmed and undermined, you're supposed to be dead, buried, broken in a corner.

But you're still standing.

You have fought bears and lions—and yet you're still standing.

You have fought giants and kings—and yet you're still standing.

You have fought temptation and darkness—and yet you're still standing.

You have fought hell itself—and yet you're still standing!

You should not have won any of those fights, let alone all of them. But in every one of those battles, you're still standing.

You have been anointed to keep standing.

You have been anointed to prove hell wrong!

Your faith has a five-stone foundation of identity, intimacy, integrity, influence, and innovation. You cannot be shaken from your faith. You cannot be defeated by the devil.

Lift up your voice and tell the world, "I'm still standing!"

Selecting Your Stone

Through the power of your anointing in the Holy Spirit, your faith is built upon the rock. You have overcome so much already in your life, and against all odds you're still standing. As you grow and mature in your faith, you are learning to rest in the sacred security of trusting God for more and bigger dreams. You know that you can withstand any storm because your five-stone foundation is unshakable. As you reflect on the power of this message, use the questions below to embrace a deeper understanding, appreciation, and application of the Spirit's power in your life.

Then take a few moments to focus on your breathing. Close your eyes, turn off your phone, and eliminate as many distractions as possible. Still your heart before the Lord and offer Him your praise and thanksgiving. Listen for the whisper of the Holy Spirit's voice and His illumination on your next steps.

1. When you consider how you're building your life on a five-stone foundation of truth, what feelings rise up inside? How has your anointing helped you construct a life of power and purpose for God's Kingdom?

2. What are some of the storms, giants, and valleys that have tried to shake the foundation of your faith? How has persevering through them in the power of your anointing made you stronger?

3. Which of the five spiritually symbolic stones—identity, intimacy, integrity, influence, innovation—is currently providing the bedrock support you need for life's storms? Which of these five stones would you like to explore in more depth as a structural support for your faith?

Dear Lord, thank You for being my Rock of Ages, my resurrected Savior whose tomb was empty after the stone was rolled away. Show me the gaps between my beliefs and my behaviors, and help me close those gaps so that my faith is reflected by my words and my deeds. Sustain my strength, stamina, and stability as I build my life on the bedrock foundation of Your truth. I should not be here considering all the lions and bears, storms and winds, giants and valleys that I've encountered—but I'm still standing, all because of You. I give You all my thanks and praise, and may everything I do give You glory. In Jesus' name, Amen.

15

Ridiculous Rewards

Enjoying Abundance in Your Glorious Future

When you live in the fullness of your anointing, you can expect a season of ridiculous rewards, redemptive unity, and righteous reputation!

A good deed is its own reward.

Virtue is its own reward.

Crossing the finish line is its own reward.

You may have your own favorite expression about what is its own reward. All of them implicitly assume, though, that expecting a reward beyond completing a good deed, virtuous act, or endurance race is more than we should hope to receive. Completing something because you're motivated by the incentive of a reward seems almost shameful for some people nowadays.

While winning competitions, comparisons, and contests can become too important for some people, our culture of the past couple decades has shifted toward recognizing and rewarding participation and not superior achievement. Instead of naming the winner of a prestigious award, the presenter at the podium announces, "The award goes to . . ."

Apparently, the thinking seems to be that naming winners inherently identifies everyone else as losers. And, of course, no one wants to be a loser.

Instead of winners and losers then, anyone who participates is applauded. School sports offer a "team trophy" to any student on the team regardless of their amount of playing time and performance. Essay contests showcase the entries of all applicants to avoid comparing, evaluating, and elevating one above the rest. Even state fairs are reluctant to declare some local baker's homemade pie a winner over the other entrants. Instead, everyone gets a blue ribbon for entering and presumably a slice of pie!

The pressure to win, to be first, to be the best at all costs can certainly be unhealthy and even toxic. This mindset persists in most every field of endeavor—even ministry. When I attend pastors' conferences, leadership seminars, and spiritual retreats, I am still surprised at the number of people who "humble brag" about how their attendance has grown, their numbers of new believers have jumped, their resources have increased, and their facilities have expanded. I understand the human tendency to compare, but I also believe ministry transcends anything we can do in our own power. We should not elevate one church over another. We should elevate all churches within the Body of Christ!

Nonetheless, being motivated by the incentive to receive a reward should not carry shame or stigma. This doesn't mean that we should compare and compete with other followers of Jesus based on human metrics. It means that we should focus on helping one another experience the radical, ridiculous rewards of righteousness promised in God's Word!

Relish the Rewards

I can think of no more fitting way to conclude this book than to consider the rewards of living in the fullness of our anointing. While we never have to compete, work, or perform for our salvation and anointing, we should relish the rewards promised to us by our loving Father, our compassionate Savior, and our powerful gift of the Holy Spirit. Embracing the anticipation of rewards beyond our imaginations provides powerful incentive to persevere.

We certainly see this in the life of David. You may recall that after his first anointing, his father, Jesse, sent him to the battlefront to take food supplies, check in with his three older brothers, and receive an update on how the battle with the pagan Philistines was progressing (see 1 Samuel 17:17–19). When David arrived, he couldn't miss the nearly ten-foot-tall warrior taunting and terrorizing the entire army of Israel and its king, Saul.

Observing this dire situation, David immediately had three questions: What's the reward for defeating this giant? Who is this guy? And why are you all tolerating his abuse? These aren't surprising questions, but the order in which David asked them might be for many of us. David begins his battle with the benefits in mind:

> Now the Israelites had been saying, "Do you see how this man [Goliath] keeps coming out? He comes out to defy Israel. The king will give great wealth to the man who kills him. He will also give him his daughter in marriage and will exempt his family from taxes in Israel."
>
> David asked the men standing near him, "What will be done for the man who kills this Philistine and removes this disgrace from Israel? Who is this uncircumcised Philistine that he should defy the armies of the living God?"
>
> They repeated to him what they had been saying and told him, "This is what will be done for the man who kills him."
>
> 1 Samuel 17:25–27

As familiar as this story remains for many people, particularly if they grew up in church, many have never considered that David was motivated to kill Goliath for the reward. While this was not his only motive, or perhaps not his primary motive, David understandably wanted to know the benefits of going to battle against such a formidable foe.

David stood motivated by righteous indignation. He stood motivated by his love and devotion for God. But David was likewise motivated by a reward—and this is not only acceptable but anointed.

It's more than okay to expect a reward for standing up for righteousness. When Jesus is your Lord, when Jesus is your Savior, when Jesus is your everything, when you are defined by the finished work of Christ and the indwelling of the Holy Spirit, you are rewarded both on this side and on the other side of eternity. You are graciously guaranteed rewards as part of your salvation.

You certainly shouldn't take my word for it—take God's Word! Throughout the New Testament, we're informed and reminded of what awaits us on the next side of eternity after our life on earth has passed. Jesus told His followers, "Rejoice and be glad, because great is your reward in heaven" (Matthew 5:12). The Lord communicated to John in his apocalyptic vision, "Look, I am coming soon! My reward is with me, and I will give to each person according to what they have done" (Revelation 22:12). James also assures us, "Blessed is the one who perseveres under trial because, having stood the test, that person will receive the crown of life that the Lord has promised to those who love him" (James 1:12).

While our eternal reward is undeniable, we also have rewards promised to us on this side of heaven. Notice how the psalmist conveys this. "For the LORD God is our sun and our shield. He gives us grace and glory. The LORD will withhold no good thing from those who do what is right" (Psalm 84:11 NLT). The wisdom collected in Proverbs also stresses what we can expect as our reward for righteousness in this life. "True humility and fear of the LORD lead to riches, honor, and long life" (Proverbs 22:4 NLT). And the corollary of this promise, "If the righteous is repaid on earth, how much more the wicked and the sinner!" (Proverbs 11:31 ESV).

Jesus repeatedly informed His followers of their reward, saying, "Seek the Kingdom of God above all else, and live righteously, and he will give you everything you need" (Matthew 6:33 NLT). He also explained that we would be rewarded through multiplied restoration of what we had lost. "And everyone who has given up houses or brothers or sisters or father or mother or children or property, for my sake, will receive a hundred times as much in return and will inherit eternal life" (Matthew 19:29 NLT). Knowing that we will be rewarded can also help motivate us to persevere when we grow weary. "So let's not get tired of doing what is good. At just the right time we will reap a harvest of blessing if we don't give up" (Galatians 6:9 NLT). Expecting a reward in this life and the next comes with your anointing!

David fought Goliath because he was anointed.

David fought Goliath because he was a man after God's own heart.

David fought Goliath because he knew God rewards the righteous.

David had expectation of a reward.

Yes, we are saved by grace through faith.

Yes, there is no greater reward than eternal, new, and abundant life.

But the Bible teaches us to expect greater things!

So you should expect your family to be saved.

Expect healing, holiness, health, and happiness.

Expect an increase.

Expect open heavens.

Expect divine favor.

Expect what money cannot buy.

I prophesy, decree, and believe that this is your season of righteous reward!

For every father and husband, brother and son, for every mother and daughter, sister and wife, for every pastor, for every influencer, for every societal architect, cultural reformer, and revivalist, no matter who you are and where you are—get ready!

Get ready for overflow.

Get ready for abundant rain.

Get ready for your cup to run over.

Get ready for exceedingly abundantly above all.

If you believe it, shout like you believe it.

If you believe it, praise like you believe it.

If you believe it, pray like you believe it.

If you believe it, live like you believe it.

Anointed in the Spirit, expect ridiculous rewards!

Dispelling Discord, Promoting Peace

In addition to the rewards of righteousness, your anointing also equips you to transcend discord and foster unity. Since the time that Adam and Eve disobeyed God in the Garden of Eden, there has been discord among human beings. Both throughout the Bible and across the pages of human history, people inevitably struggle to get along. When you're living in the fullness of your anointing, however, you promote peace rather than perpetuate problems. Even when other people attack, assault, comment, criticize, troll, and try to pick a fight with you, your anointing facilitates faith and unity rather than animosity and division.

Discord often becomes a way for the enemy to attempt a distraction from the battle we know we must fight. This was certainly the case with David—and from his own family, no less.

> But when David's oldest brother, Eliab, heard David talking to the men, he was angry. "What are you doing around here anyway?" he demanded. "What about those few sheep you're supposed to be taking care of? I know about your pride and deceit. You just want to see the battle!"
>
> 1 Samuel 17:28 NLT

It's one thing not to receive support, encouragement, and affirmation in the battles you fight. But it's another thing when the dissonance of others' disdain compounds the challenge! David's brothers falsely accused him of selfish, egotistical motives.

Just think about this situation for a moment. The enemy of Israel stood before them all, mocking and threatening them and their God, and yet David's brothers preoccupied themselves with attacking the character of the only person brave enough to take on their enemy—who just happened to be their younger brother!

I have no doubt you have experienced this dynamic in your own battles as well. You step out in faith, you step up to the problem, and you get stepped on! Someone puts you down for trying to be the center of attention, for trying to show off and show up everyone else. Someone assumes the worst about you right at the time your anointing is bringing out and empowering your best.

And as much as it pains me to raise the question, is this not the problem with the Church today? I fear that we spend more time attacking, insulting, and criticizing each other than we do focusing on the giants that stand threatening us. We go around pointing our fingers at the specks in other people's eyes rather than addressing the planks obstructing our own vision. We lose the big eternal picture and nitpick on irrelevant details and individual flaws.

Understand, though, that this is precisely what the enemy wants us to do. He's determined to accumulate the forces of darkness in hopes of blinding us and sowing weeds of discord in order to destroy our spiritual fruit. Some dark forces are recognizable, but when they all come together, the result can leave us in a fog of uncertainty, doubt, distraction, and apathy.

The dark forces of moral relativism, of cultural decadence, of spiritual apathy, of hedonism and perversion, of socialism, communism, and Marxism, of atheism and Gnosticism have all come together in order to silence forever more our Judeo-Christian worldview that serves as the firewall against the gates of hell.

In the meantime, the Church has been divided. Today, it often looks like donkeys versus elephants, partisan versus independents, Fox News versus CNN, charismatic versus automatic, Catholics versus Protestants, denomination versus denomination, egalitarianism versus complementarianism, or dispensationalism versus "occupy until He comes."

But I'm here to tell you, in the power of your anointing, you can be a peacemaker, a unifier, a healer, and a grace-giver. In the power of your anointing, you become spiritual superglue, demonstrating the prayer Jesus prayed to His Father.

> As you sent me into the world, I have sent them into the world. For them I sanctify myself, that they too may be truly sanctified.
>
> My prayer is not for them alone. I pray also for those who will believe in me through their message, that all of them may be one, Father, just as you are in me and I am in you. May they also be in us so that the world may believe that you have sent me. I have given them the glory that you gave me, that they may be one as we are one—I in them and

> you in me—so that they may be brought to complete unity. Then the world will know that you sent me and have loved them even as you have loved me.
>
> John 17:18–23

How do I know you are fulfilling this prayer? Because if our heavenly Father does not answer Jesus' prayer, we are all in bad shape! Jesus came so that we might be one with God. He is the vine and we are the branches (see John 15:5). Through Him we have life and are united through the blood of the cross and the love of the Father.

Jesus prayed, "Father, make them one as you and I are one." Living in our anointing, you and I are being called to answer our Lord's request. I'm convinced we are about to see a unity movement in the Church. The Church is coming together. New life, new union, new wholeness will characterize the Body of Christ. Just like the prophet Ezekiel, I hear the sound of rattling bones coming together. "So I spoke this message, just as he told me. Suddenly as I spoke, there was a rattling noise all across the valley. The bones of each body came together and attached themselves as complete skeletons" (Ezekiel 37:7 NLT). When the Body comes together, giants will fall!

The giant of unholy hedonism will come down when the Church comes together.

The giant of workaholism will come down when the Church comes together.

The giant of financial greed will come down when the Church comes together.

The giant of moral relativism will come down with the Church comes together.

Let us pray together, "Lord, make us holy, make us one, make us light!"

Your Righteous Reputation

When you live in the fullness of your anointing in God's Spirit, you establish a righteous reputation. This blessing often results from the other two major benefits—your righteous rewards and others' awareness of how you facilitate redemptive unity. Keep in mind, too, that cultivating a righteous reputation doesn't result just from the testimony of God's presence in your life that others witness. Your righteous reputation also arises from your awareness of how God has used your past battles to prepare and equip you for the next one.

Despite the false assumptions and unmerited criticism of his brothers, David proceeded to fight Goliath only to encounter another obstacle—the perception of those in authority that David lacked experience and was therefore unqualified to even attempt taking on such a powerful adversary.

> "Don't worry about this Philistine," David told Saul. "I'll go fight him!"
>
> "Don't be ridiculous!" Saul replied. "There's no way you can fight this Philistine and possibly win! You're only a boy, and he's been a man of war since his youth."
>
> But David persisted. "I have been taking care of my father's sheep and goats," he said. "When a lion or a bear comes to steal a lamb from the flock, I go after it with a club and rescue the lamb from its mouth. If the animal turns on me, I catch it by the jaw and club it to death. I have done this to both lions and bears, and I'll do it to this pagan Philistine, too, for he has defied the armies of the living God! The LORD who rescued me from the claws of the lion and the bear will rescue me from this Philistine!"
>
> Saul finally consented. "All right, go ahead," he said. "And may the LORD be with you!"
>
> 1 Samuel 17:32–37 NLT

The king, too terrified to confront the enemy of his nation, doubted anyone could conquer the Philistine giant, let alone someone as unlikely, untrained, and inexperienced as the naive teen insisting his right to fight. And the basis for David's confidence? David qualified himself by his testimony.

In essence, David said, "What I fought in the past has prepared me for this hour!"

His record spoke for itself. "I defeated the lion and the bear. If they stole what belonged to me, I pursued them. If they turned toward me,

I took away their ability to bite, rip, tear, or devour. How? By grabbing their jaw and swinging my club!"

Did anyone see David conquer the bear and the lion? No!

What you overcome in private will enable you to triumph in public.

Your reputation for righteousness results from the unique spiritual confidence that comes from humility and holiness. You know you cannot succeed on your own, so you rely on the power of the Spirit through your anointing. Because you know the source of your power, you rush toward the obstacles, the giants, and the enemies before you.

On your journey toward victory, others will want to assume they know you—and therefore know that you really don't have what it takes. You're too young or too old, too inexperienced or overqualified, too educated or not educated enough, too flexible or too rigid, too reliant on technology or too resistant to it. Those in authority often find some reason for minimizing, undermining, and discounting your courageous contribution. Which is why you must tell them, "You don't know me!"

You think you know me, but you don't know me.

You know what you've seen, and you know what you've heard.

You know what my brothers have said about me. But you don't know me.

You think you know me because you've read my posts on Facebook and Instagram.

You assume you know who I am because of what you have read on Wikipedia and LinkedIn.

But you don't know me.

You don't know the bears and the lions I've fought to get here.

You don't know the giants I've toppled along my path.

You don't know the devils and demons I've had to cast out.

You don't know the nights I've prayed, fasted, and prophesied.

You don't know the battles I've fought and the obstacles I've overcome.

You don't know the generational curses I've broken.

Here's all that others need to know—you're anointed by the power of the Holy Spirit to prove hell wrong! Just like David, through the finished work of Jesus, you are anointed to enjoy the abundance of ridiculous rewards, redemptive unity, and righteous reputation.

Your testimony is greater than your trauma.

Your destiny is greater than your drama.

Your praise is greater than your pain.

Your battle scars are your credentials.

You know what it is to fight for your sheep.

You know what it means to fight for your dream.

You know what it means to fight for your faith.

You overcame by the blood of the Lamb and the word of your testimony.

Your private battles forge a righteous reputation that qualifies you for public triumph.

What you overcame before now becomes your testimony to slay giants!

Like David, you are anointed by the Spirit of God. In the fullness of your anointing, you claim the fullness of a five-stone faith and anticipate rewards in this life and the next. In the fullness of your anointing, you promote peace and redemptive unity in the midst of discord and division. In the fullness of your anointing, your reputation is righteousness!

From strength to strength, you grow stronger and stronger as God continues to amplify your anointing. There is no giant you cannot defeat, no valley you cannot climb, no storm you cannot endure. Goliath never wins. Because your identity, your intimacy, your integrity, your influence, and your innovation equip you for the abundant joy of your anointing!

You are spiritually and strategically empowered to slay your giants!

Selecting Your Stone

As you conclude our exploration of living in the fullness of your anointing in God's Spirit, use these final questions to reflect on all you've learned from engaging with the message of each chapter. Consider how your relationship with God, particularly the Holy Spirit within you, has grown and changed since you started reading this book. Spend some time in prayer thanking God for all He's revealing to you and for all the ways He will continue to lead you into the fullness of your anointing in His Spirit. To God be the glory!

1. As you consider your reading experience, what has had the greatest impact on your relationship with the Lord? What has changed in the way you understand and relate to the Holy Spirit within you?

2. What has the Spirit within you revealed about your God-given purpose and how you're being prepared, equipped, and guided to fulfill it? What are your next steps in continuing to fulfill your anointed mission in this life?

3. Which of the ridiculous rewards of righteousness resonate the most with you right now? How does knowing all that God has promised to you motivate you to live more fully in the power of the Holy Spirit?

Dear God, there is no way for me to express my thanks, gratitude, and appreciation for the gift of Your anointing in the Holy Spirit other than to love You, live for You, and serve others in Your holy name. Empower me to grow in my reliance on Your Spirit, to cultivate patience rather than rushing ahead in my own power, and to enjoy the full abundance of blessings and benefits You bestow on me. May I bring glory to You, Lord, as I pursue fulfilling the divine purpose for which You created me. I praise You and worship You for Your goodness, Your grace, and Your generosity. In Jesus' name, Amen.

SAMUEL RODRIGUEZ is president of the National Hispanic Christian Leadership Conference (NHCLC), the world's largest Hispanic Christian organization, with more than 42,000 United States churches and many additional churches spread throughout the Spanish-speaking diaspora.

Rodriguez stands recognized by CNN, Fox News, Univision, and Telemundo as America's most influential Latino/Hispanic faith leader. *Charisma Magazine* named him one of the forty leaders who changed the world. *The Wall Street Journal* named him one of the top twelve Latino leaders, and he was the only faith leader on that list. He has been named among the "Top 100 Christian Leaders in America" (Newsmax 2018) and nominated as one of the "100 Most Influential People in the World" (Time 2013). Rodriguez is regularly featured on CNN, Fox News, Univision, PBS, *Christianity Today*, *The New York Times*, *The Wall Street Journal*, and many others.

Rodriguez was the first Latino to deliver the keynote address at the annual Martin Luther King Jr. Commemorative Service at Ebenezer Baptist Church, and he is a recipient of the Martin Luther King Jr. Leadership Award presented by the Congress of Racial Equality.

Rodriguez advised American presidents Bush, Obama, and Trump, and he frequently consults with Congress regarding advancing immigration and criminal justice reform as well as religious freedom and pro-life initiatives. By the grace of God, the Rev. Samuel Rodriguez is one of the few individuals to have participated in the inauguration ceremonies of two different presidents representing both political parties.

In January 2009, Pastor Sam read from the gospel of Luke for Mr. Obama's inaugural morning service at Saint John's Episcopal Church. On January 20, 2017, at Mr. Trump's inauguration, with more than one billion people watching from around the world, Pastor Sam became the first Latino evangelical to participate in a U.S. presidential inaugural ceremony, reading from Matthew 5 and concluding with "in Jesus' name!" In April 2020, Reverend Rodriguez was appointed to the National Coronavirus Recovery Commission to offer specialized experience and expertise in crisis mitigation and recovery to help national, state, and local leaders guide America through the COVID-19 pandemic.

Rodriguez is the executive producer of two films: *Breakthrough*, the GMA Dove Award winner for Inspirational Film of the Year, with an Academy Award nomination for Best Original Song, and *Flamin' Hot*, in partnership with Franklin Entertainment and 20th Century Fox. He is also co-founder of TBN Salsa, an international Christian-based broadcast television network, and he is the author of *You Are Next*, *Shake Free*, *Be Light*—a number one *Los Angeles Times* bestseller—and *From Survive to Thrive*, a number one Amazon bestseller.

He earned his master's degree from Lehigh University and has received honorary doctorates from Northwest University, William Jessup University, and Baptist University of the Americas.

Rodriguez serves as the senior pastor of New Season Church, one of America's fastest- growing megachurches and number thirteen on "Newsmax's Top 50 Megachurches in America," with campuses in Los Angeles and Sacramento, California, where he resides with his wife, Eva, and their three children.

For more information:

PastorSam.com

RevSamuelRodriguez

@PastorSamuelRodriguez

@NHCLC